"Steve Strauss has been helping small business succeed for more than 20 years and he does it again in *Your Small Business Boom*. You would be smart to follow his advice."

Brian Moran
CEO, Small Business Edge

"There's few people who know about small business success like Steve. This book is SO needed, especially now!"

Ramon Ray
global speaker and founder of SmartHustle.com

"Small business expert, mentor, strategist, advisor, and friend. Steve is all those things. When you read *Your Small Business Boom* and apply his tips, you too will be able to take your business to the next level."

Laurel Delaney
founder of GlobeTrade.com and President of
Women Entrepreneurs Grow Global

"I first met Steve Strauss when he began at *USA TODAY* and I was the editorial director of *Entrepreneur* magazine. In the years since, I have always been impressed with, not only all of the various ways he helps small businesses (his column, books, speeches, etc.), but even more so, how he can convey so many valuable ideas in an easy-to-understand, fun way. *Your Small Business Boom* is the latest (and maybe best) example of this. I love this book and bet you will too!"

Rieva Lesonsky
CEO, President and founder at GrowBiz Media

YOUR SMALL BUSINESS BOOM

EXPLOSIVE IDEAS

TO GROW YOUR BUSINESS,
MAKE MORE MONEY,
AND THRIVE IN A VOLATILE WORLD

STEVEN D. STRAUSS

Mc Graw Hill

New York Chicago San Francisco Athens London Madrid
Mexico City Milan New Delhi Singapore Sydney Toronto

1 2 3 4 5 6 7 8 9   LCR   26 25 24 23 22 21

ISBN   978-1-264-26661-6
MHID   1-264-26661-8

e-ISBN 978-1-264-26662-3
e-MHID   1-264-26662-6

Library of Congress Cataloging-in-Publication Data

Names: Strauss, Steven D., 1958- author.
Title: Your small business boom : explosive ideas to grow your business, make
    more money, and thrive in a volatile world / Steven D. Strauss.
Description: New York : McGraw Hill, 2022. | Includes bibliographical
    references and index.
Identifiers: LCCN 2021024517 (print) | LCCN 2021024518 (ebook) |
    ISBN 9781264266616 (hardcover) | ISBN 9781264266623 (ebook)
Subjects: LCSH: Small business—Management. | Small business—Finance. |
    New business enterprises.
Classification: LCC HD62.7 .S876 2022 (print) | LCC HD62.7 (ebook) |
    DDC 658.02/2—dc23
LC record available at https://lccn.loc.gov/2021024517
LC ebook record available at https://lccn.loc.gov/2021024518

McGraw Hill books are available at special quantity discounts to use as premiums and sales promotions or for use in corporate training programs. To contact a representative, please visit the Contact Us pages at www.mhprofessional.com.

This book is dedicated to my kind, funny, smart, generous wife, Maria. Thank you for making all things possible.

CONTENTS

ACKNOWLEDGMENTS

First, thank you to my new/old friend and agent, Gary Krebs, without whom this book would not be. I have had several agents over the years, but none as good or as dedicated as you. This is my eighteenth book, and you were there at the beginning. Chai!

Thanks also to my fantastic research assistant Kieran Yancy, who made my job of writing this book so much easier with his excellent efforts and spot-on research.

Thanks as well to my new teammates at McGraw Hill for having the vision.

Finally, much love and thanks to my great brothers Larry and Spence, to my beloved mom, Sandi Strauss, to my great dad, Marty Strauss, and to my very special second dad, Seymour Fagan. And, as always, none of this would be possible without the love and support of Maria, Jillian, Sydney, and Mara. Always and forever in my heart.

FOREWORD

've spent my career helping small businesses succeed, and so Steve Strauss and I have that in common.

That's good news for you.

In my CNBC show *The Profit* and throughout all areas of my work, I seek out struggling small businesses to invest in, advise, and turn around. What I love is when I find businesses with a lot of potential—the ones that just need some fresh ideas and a nudge in a new direction. I know that if those entrepreneurs work with me and are willing to learn something new, together we cannot only make a lot of money and have some fun, but make a difference, too.

And that is what Steve Strauss and *Your Small Business Boom* are all about.

Throughout this book, you'll see Steve's passion for, and commitment to, small businesses and entrepreneurs. He wants to make a difference for you and for your business. Whether it is some very clever digital marketing strategies, or how to make social media *really* work for your business, or simply the power of good, old-fashioned networking and teamwork, this very valuable and easy to follow book shows you how to take your business (whatever its current size) to the next level.

While I've grown Camping World to a company listed on the New York Stock Exchange, it wasn't always so. I began my career as an entrepreneur of a much, much smaller business, but through hard work, teamwork, and my commitment to what I call the

Three Ps (People, Process, and Product), we were able to significantly grow.

Your Small Business Boom will give you tools to help you do the same. What I know is that having great teammates and mentors makes all the difference on your business journey, and that is what I really think Steve is offering you in this book.

Read on. It's time to make more profit!

Marcus Lemonis
Entrepreneur and CNBC's *The Profit*

INTRODUCTION

Break on through to the other side!
—Jim Morrison, The Doors

Wow.

No one saw that coming.

To say that the COVID-19 pandemic affected our lives in ways both large and small would be a vast understatement. Businesses shuttered and entrepreneurs shuddered.

While various programs helped and while customers did their best to support their favorite small businesses, it is equally true that nothing really was the same after COVID-19 hit. How could it be? Many small businesses went out of business, others clung on, and yet others boomed. It was an upside-down world.

And as the world returns to normal, it's evident that the pandemic left behind a changed landscape—physically, emotionally, and economically—and in that change, there is an opportunity for something new, and—dare we say?—better.

That growth can and should include your small business.

You can create your own small business boom.

That's what this book is about—how to take advantage of this emerging new reality and take your business to the next level.

Doesn't that sound great? Instead of being stuck doing the same thing you have been doing, you can do something new, bigger, and better. That something is out there, waiting for you. With some new ideas and strategies, a little work, some creativity, a few new skills, and a heaping teaspoon of attitude, you can take your business to the next level.

This book is for you if:

- You are looking to *really* grow your business
- You are a small business wanting to make more money, a lot more money
- You want to master the digital universe, and/or
- You are looking for truly powerful ways to kick things up a notch (or two or three!)

These are not idle boasts or promises. Helping people start, run, grow, and succeed in their own businesses is what I do. It is my passion. My purpose. It is my commitment to you. It is also my experience. I have been an entrepreneur my whole adult life, having started three very successful businesses. I have also been the lead small business columnist for *USA TODAY* for over 20 years, and was named the top small business champion in the country by the country's leading small business organization. I have a six-figure social media following and have worked with many, many entrepreneurs and small business owners, helping them create their own small business boom.

I tell you all this not to impress you, but to impress upon you that what you have in your hands is what you have been look-ing for—the secret sauces used by some of the world's best, most successful entrepreneurs, seven-figure solopreneurs, and small businesses of all sizes in between. *Businesses and people like you!*

These are the ideas, strategies, tips, and tricks that work now, today.

I used one of the strategies in this book to quadruple my income in less than two years. Another was taught to me by an entrepreneur who used it to create an opt-in list of some 500,000 people. With that list, he nets millions a year from new product launches. There are scores of similarly powerful, viable, affordable, easy-to-implement business growth strategies throughout this book.

Read the book. Find some ideas you like. Try them on for size. See what works. See what doesn't. If I did my job right, finding a few workable strategies that can boom your business should not be all that difficult, and the benefits *can literally be life changing.*

It is like this: In the movie *The Edge*, Alec Baldwin and Anthony Hopkins play two men whose small plane crashes in the Alaskan outback. They have no provisions, no tools save for a jack-knife and a small book Hopkins had brought along called *How to Survive in the Wild.*

And wouldn't you know it, soon enough, the two men need the book because they are being stalked by a Kodiak bear and have to figure out how to survive in the wild. Baldwin's character is petrified, convinced they will die at the hands of the bear. But not Hopkins. His little book has a chapter entitled "How to Kill a Bear." While Hopkins is convinced they can do it, Baldwin balks.

"What one man can do, another can do!" Hopkins tells Baldwin. "If someone else figured out how to kill a bear, then we can too. Now say it after me—What one person can do, another can do, too!" Hopkins bellows.

Baldwin can't bring himself to say it. He doesn't believe it. But Hopkins will not be dismissed. "Say it after me—What one man can do, another can do!" Baldwin's character has no choice, and before long, he not only begins to say it, he actually begins to believe it.

"What one man can do, another can do!" he finally yells.

You know how the story has to end, right? With the bear on their trail, the men are tested to their limit. The bear finally attacks, and Hopkins and Baldwin lift the crude spears they have whittled to try to fend it off. But the bear is in a frenzy. It gets inches from their faces, but as it does, the giant beast makes a wrong move, impales itself on their spears, and crumples to the ground, dead.

I often tell small businesses that they do not have to reinvent the wheel. Someone or some entrepreneur or some small business or some large company has already figured out how to kill the bear (as it were). They have spent considerable time, money, effort, and resources learning and perfecting what works. All we need to do is discover what those things are and copy them.

So that is what we are going to do.

What one person can do, another can do.

We got this!

Steve Strauss
MrAllBiz.com

PART I

PIVOT AND GROW RICH

In this new world, the opportunity for small businesses of all sizes to grow is emerging. In this section, you will find six powerful strategies for taking your business to the next level.

THE PIVOT

If I go there will be trouble
And if I stay it will be double
—The Clash

Whether or not we like it or wanted it, change has been thrust upon us these past few years. Between COVID-19, quarantining, the ensuing economic crash, unrelenting unemployment, businesses shuttering, the massive pivot online, and now, rebirth, our personal and business lives were completely upended.

Yet, while a pandemic was not remotely on our collective radar, change definitely should have been. The dot-com bubble bursting at the turn of the century changed the world, as did 9/11 shortly thereafter. A few years later, in 2008, what I call the "Not-So-Great Recession" almost became a new Great Depression. That same year, the first African American was elected president, and yet eight years later, Donald Trump succeeded him.

And that's the thing. Change happens.

Given that, the Clash seem to have put it best: If you stay where you are, your trouble will double. Rather than resisting the inevitable change that we clearly constantly live with, it behooves us to accept the reality that the only constant is change. As such, it is far better to surf the change wave than to turn your back and have it crash on you.

MASTER CHANGE,
OR IT WILL MASTER YOU

In what is widely considered the greatest Star Trek movie of all time, *Star Trek II: The Wrath of Khan*, cadets must pass a seemingly no-win test. In it, a starship named the *Kobayashi Maru* is stuck in the Neutral Zone, a place in the cosmos where travel is forbidden. If a Star Fleet commander decides to attempt a rescue of the vessel, it will start a war with the Klingons, but if he or she does nothing, the crew of the *Kobayashi Maru* will surely die. It's a lose-lose scenario.

Of course, the only cadet ever to pass the test was James T. Kirk. How? The soon-to-be Captain Kirk surreptitiously reprograms Star Fleet's computer so that a third option—a safe rescue—is possible. Though technically cheating, Kirk is nevertheless awarded an accommodation for "original thinking."

Original thinking is what we must do too if we want to grow our businesses in spite of these perilous times.

Take, for instance, my colleague Jeff. At the start of the Great Recession in 2008, Jeff was faced with his own *Kobayashi Maru* nightmare scenario. Jeff owned a very successful, million-dollar software consulting company; his team of about two dozen employees installed and serviced sophisticated business software on their small business clients' computer systems. Times were good, business was thriving, and Jeff never saw the economic tsunami of 2008 coming. But suddenly, the bottom fell out of the housing market, the stock market crashed, clients canceled contracts, Jeff's business hit a wall, and revenue evaporated.

Sound familiar?

Like Captain Kirk, Jeff was seemingly faced with choices bad and worse. He could:

- Let everyone go, close up shop, and retire, or
- Let almost everyone go and run a lean shop for a few years, or maybe forever

Neither option was very appealing. But also like Captain Kirk, Jeff realized he could opt for original thinking. Getting creative, he realized that he actually had a third option: *He could create a virtual business.*

This was a radical notion at a time, long before the pandemic, when remote work was the exception and not the rule. One thing Jeff knew was that to survive, he would have to radically reduce his overhead. Traditionally, the way to do this is by firing people since labor is such a major expense for most businesses. But Jeff also knew that *his team was his business.* Instead, his eureka idea was that he should eliminate his office space, not his people.

> Martha Stewart's first business was as a caterer in Connecticut. One night while catering an event for a publisher in New York, she got to talking to one of the executives. He loved her food, and they discussed the possibility of having her write a cookbook.
>
> It took five years, but eventually Martha Stewart's *Entertaining* was published and became a hit. But it was her bold, original thinking that started the Martha Stewart empire. She did not name her new company *Martha Stewart Catering* or *Martha Stewart Entertainment*, but rather, *Martha Stewart Living Omnimedia*, a company that would eventually include books, a magazine, television shows, and websites.

So that is what he did. Jeff got out of his lease, closed the office, and had his team begin to work from home. Soon, they figured out some processes. They met virtually daily and physically weekly. And it worked. Not only did they survive that horrible recession, but these days, Jeff's business is doing better than ever. Revenues hit new highs in 2019, and his staff has grown.

More importantly for our purposes, when the economic tsunami named COVID-19 hit, Jeff was ready. Unlike so many small businesses, Jeff had seen the future of business, and its name was virtual.

Because of this, rather than wreaking havoc on his business, the pandemic had the opposite effect. With so many small businesses having to up their online game during COVID-19, the need for Jeff's cloud solutions multiplied, and since his team already worked virtually, the pandemic had little negative effect on his operations.

Instead, business boomed.

DON'T LET A GOOD CRISIS GO TO WASTE

Jeff's story serves as a valuable lesson in how to "not let a good crisis go to waste." You have heard of that saying, right? It was first uttered by British Prime Minister Winston Churchill near the end of World War II. There is no need to belabor the tragedy that was the Second World War except to say that the struggles people individually and collectively went through laid the foundation for a far better postwar world. That is what is critical for our purposes, for *your* purposes.

A crisis can birth a new, bigger, better beginning.

In the case of the war, Churchill and the other powers that be (President Franklin Roosevelt, etc.) knew that out of the wreckage of the war, a better world was possible—*if* they didn't squander the opening (physical, political, economic, psychological) that resulted from the crisis they had just surmounted. They knew you can't let a good crisis go to waste.

We are now, here, today, again at such an inflection point, only the thing is that for you and me, the opportunity of which Churchill spoke is not geopolitical, it is not macroeconomic, it is personal, it is entrepreneurial.

About 15 years later, in 1959, John F. Kennedy had something eerily similar to say at a speech in Indianapolis, "The Chinese use two brushstrokes to write the word 'crisis.' One brush stroke stands for danger; the other for opportunity. In a crisis, be aware of the danger—but recognize the opportunity."

Indeed, in 2020, none other than Mark Cuban noted, "When we look back at the pandemic in 20 years, we're going to recognize that there were 20, 30 or more world-class companies that changed the game and that there was a lot of creative destruction where we saw business go by the wayside to make room for new ones." What does that mean for you? Says Cuban, "I think this is a phenomenal time to create new opportunities in business. I don't think there's a better time ever to start a company."[1]

Changes are afoot. Phenomenal opportunities—in all sorts of surprising forms—abound.

THE REMOTE WORK REVOLUTION

The obvious first change that can make your small business life better, easier, and more profitable stems from the advent of remote work as a mainstay in our work life. Remote work in some form is here to stay, and it makes a heck of a lot of sense to embrace it.

Here's why: It is difficult to say which is more surprising—that a once-in-a-century pandemic forced millions of companies to create a remote workplace or that, as the pandemic began to subside, millions of their workers chose to continue working from home, saying that they were happier and more productive that way.

In fact, according to the World Economic Forum, "In a McKinsey survey of 800 corporate executives around the world, 38% of the respondents expected their remote employees to continue working from home one or two days a week after the pandemic."[2] Indeed, going forward, there are some very real reasons why adopting some hybrid model of in and out of the office—is the smart way to go:

Employee happiness. Workers who are given the flexibility to work from home tend to be happier and more productive. In 2019, the video conferencing company Owl Labs surveyed 1,200 workers for its State of Remote Work Report.[3] It found that:

- **Remote workers work more.** Remote workers said they work over 40 hours per week—43 percent more than on-site workers.
- **Remote workers are more loyal.** By 13 percent, surveyed workers said that they are more likely to stay in their current job for the next five years.
- **Remote workers are happier.** By 22 percent, full-time remote workers said they were happier in their job than people who never work remotely. Why? Work-life balance (91 percent), increased productivity (79 percent), and less stress (78 percent.)

Cost savings. Needless to say, having employees work from home, at least part-time, offers a business substantial savings in insurance, operations, and overhead.

Disaster preparedness. Many—nay most—small businesses were caught wholly unprepared for the wrath of COVID-19. Even though a pandemic was obviously a worst-case scenario, it proves that the worst case happens. That is why we have insurance. Floods, fire, theft, riots, earthquakes, and many more bad things can befall a business. By being virtual, you can lessen their impact.

Wave of the future. No one who lived through the pandemic will forget it, and that includes customers, entrepreneurs, and investors. What worked and what did not will be analyzed and dissected for years to come, and those things that did work—like remote work—will not soon be discarded. You can be one of the pioneers who paved the way for a new kind of work.

Sustainability. Creating even a hybrid physical-virtual business allows you to help the environment. Less people commuting to your office lowers your carbon footprint and is overall better for the planet. A win-win.

OPPORTUNITIES BEYOND HYBRID WORK

The remote work revolution is but one lasting change that the smart entrepreneur can use to begin to boom his or her business. There are many more emerging trends of which you can avail yourself in your quest to take things to the next level. In fact, you are holding an entire book of them. That said, one in particular needs to be highlighted up front.

New Markets

It may be ironic, but one of the best things to have happened to small business as a result of the pandemic was the massive pivot to online shopping. Now, of course, it wasn't easy and not a few businesses had a difficult time figuring out how to turn their offline, physical business into an online, virtual one. That said, many entrepreneurs were in fact quite creative and managed the trick quite adroitly.

The reason I am suggesting our change in shopping habits should be seen as fortuitous and not disastrous is that it forced many entrepreneurs to (1) re-think their business model, and (2) begin to sell online—whether they wanted to or not.

The upshot of this was that many ended up with altogether new ways to make money and grow their business—strategies that they very likely would not have considered had they not been forced to.

That's the ticket.

As you will see throughout this book, creating additional, new streams of income (both online and offline) is one of the best ways to make your business go boom.

Take, for example, Katie Kaps and her team at HigherDOSE. In 2016, Katie decided that she wanted to create a new type of spa in New York City, but as with everything in New York, she also knew it had to have a twist: it had to be unique, different, and better in order to stand out. And that is exactly what she came up with—HigherDOSE, a spa experience where infrared light was the star of the show. Not only does a bath of infrared light give you a natural high, but it is equally great for curing muscle pain and detoxifying the body of impurities. It's akin to getting the benefits of a workout without working out.

No wonder HigherDOSE spas were so popular.

But of course, what the HigherDOSE team never expected—indeed what none of us ever expected—was a pandemic. In their case, almost overnight, HigherDOSE had to shutter nine locations. What do you do when your physical, experience-based business is closed down without notice? Well, you adapt. And that is exactly what Katie and her team at HigherDOSE did.

They immediately pivoted to direct-to-consumer e-commerce, focusing on selling what had been a small piece of their business up until then—at-home infrared blankets.

It worked.

With everyone at home and stressed out, the demand for a product like the HigherDOSE infrared blanket—something that could de-stress people and give them an at-home spa experience—skyrocketed.

These days, HigherDOSE makes more money from e-commerce than they ever did with retail stores. And they did it by embracing change and doing some original thinking. Armed with some chutzpah, a positive mindset, a great idea, a good product, and some savvy digital marketing, HigherDOSE began to radiate.

Why not you, too? Opportunities abound.

With the emergence of a more flexible, affordable remote work option, with the potential for an e-commerce bonanza waiting for you out there, and with scores of lucrative new markets available that can be reached with powerful digital marketing tools, a much bigger, better, more fun, more profitable business can be yours too if you choose not to let a good crisis go to waste. Opportunities abound. If you are willing to do the opposite of those who are doing nothing, and if you embrace a post-pandemic pivot, your very own small business boom awaits.

BOOM YOUR BUSINESS BOTTOM LINE

▶ Like Captain Kirk, when faced with a *Kobayashi Maru* scenario, you too can choose a third option with some original, creative thinking.

▶ Master change or it will master you.

▶ Remote work is here to stay, and that is a good thing. Remote employees are happy employees.

▶ Lucrative opportunities abound if you refuse to let a good crisis go to waste.

CHAPTER 2

DO THE OPPOSITE

Be fearful when others are greedy
and be greedy when others are fearful.
—Warren Buffett

I n one of the funniest, but also most prescient, episodes of *Seinfeld*, the gang is sitting at the coffee shop, and George is, of course ,lamenting the sad state of his life. The waitress comes over to take their order and says to George, "Tuna on toast, coleslaw, cup of coffee?" George says yes because that is what he always orders, and then, in a bolt of bravado, declares no, because "Nothing's ever worked out for me with tuna on toast. I want the complete opposite of on toast!" And so he orders chicken salad on rye, untoasted.

Now, of course, the opposite of tuna on toast may or may not be chicken salad, but the point is the same—by doing what he has always done, George gets what he has always gotten, namely, not enough.

So George orders the opposite, and right then a beautiful woman at the counter turns and smiles at him. Elaine notices and tells George to go talk to her. George demurs. He can't, he explains to Elaine, he's bald and lives at home with his parents. Jerry retorts: "But if every instinct you have is wrong, then doing the opposite would have to be right."

George lights up. "Yes, I will do the opposite!" he announces. He gets up, saunters over to the counter, and says to her, "Hello,

13

my name is George. I am unemployed and I live with my parents." She looks up, smiles broadly and says, "Hi, I'm Victoria."

BOOMS HAPPEN

As the late, great media personality Paul Harvey once said, "In times like these, it is good to remember that there have always been times like these." Was he speaking of pandemics? No, of course not. But challenging times? You bet. And in challenging times like these it is understandable that the reaction of many small businesses is to truncate, retrench, pull back, and duck for cover. They cut overhead, reduce spending, trim the sails, and wait. Then, once the coast is clear, they will again start to slowly spend money, market tentatively, invest in training, and dig out.

Mistake, that.

Instead, what actually works is to be like George and do the opposite. Am I telling you to take a wild, crazy risk? No, of course not. But a smart, prudent risk is just what the doctor ordered if your business is to succeed and thrive in these turbulent times. Doing the same ol', same ol' will get you the same ol', same ol'.

> According to the Berkeley Well-Being Institute, "Doing the opposite of what you might normally do helps disrupt the well-worn pathways in your brain. By . . . [confusing] our brains, we begin to break up our patterns."[1]

Yes, it may seem counterintuitive, and that is because it is. After all, we do the same things the same ways over and over again often out of force of habit, but the thing is, those habits are not always the most effective. That is why deciding to do the opposite (or at least something new and different) can make such a huge difference. If you are looking to take your business to the next level, if you are looking to make more money, have more fun, cast a wider net, and make a bigger difference, then what is required is that you THINK BIG, not act small. Acting small will get you small results, safe results.

Consider what none other than Warren Buffett has to say about being bold, thinking big, and doing the opposite:

- "Those who invest only when [times] are upbeat end up paying a heavy price . . ."
- "We've put a lot of money to work during [times of] chaos. It's an ideal period for investors. A climate of fear is their best friend . . . Big opportunities come infrequently, [and so, when] it's raining gold, reach for a bucket, not a thimble."[2]

Big opportunities come infrequently, but when they do, you need to reach for a bucket, not a thimble. And that time is now. We are on the cusp of what is next, but the thing is, no one quite knows what "next" will look like; it has yet to be written. But you can write your own next right now.

Opportunity awaits. Like Warren Buffett, you can buy when everyone else is selling.

HISTORY REPEATS ITSELF

The conventional wisdom was that that the Great Recession of 2008 was not a good time to start a business. But there's a thing about the conventional wisdom: It's conventional. And no business ever boomed by being too conventional.

Fortunately, Brian Acton and Jan Koum figured that out. Right before that recession, in 2007, Acton and Koum left their cushy jobs at Yahoo. They applied for jobs at Facebook but were rejected. And so, before long, they found themselves out of work and in the middle of a recession.

They decided that it was a perfect time to start a business.

Even though this was the opposite of the conventional wisdom at the time, Acton and Koum were convinced that they had a winning idea: The iPhone was just gaining traction, and given its rising popularity, they figured that what the world needed was a better messaging app, specifically one that was safer and encoded. The problem, however, was that they themselves were unable to make it because they were not coders and they didn't know any coders. What to do?

They did what you or I might do: They jumped online, did a Google search, and found a site called RentACoder.com.

After scrolling through various profiles, the partners found and hired a Russian coder named Igor Solomennikov. They explained to him that they were looking to create an app that would be encoded and private, that users the world over could use to message one another safely and confidentially on Wi-Fi and other such "open" networks.

Solomennikov went to work and before long was able to show them a prototype of the messaging app they had envisioned. Yes, it was exactly what they were looking for. Playing off of the phrase "What's up?" the duo named it "WhatsApp."

Launched in November of 2009, WhatsApp struck a chord immediately, especially overseas. By early 2011, WhatsApp had become one of the Top 20 apps in Apple's App Store. By 2013— when the rest of the world was just starting to emerge from its recessionary-induced slumber—WhatsApp passed the 200 million subscribers mark. Today WhatsApp has more than 2 billion users.

And here's the kicker: the next year, Facebook, the company that wouldn't even hire Acton and Koum just a few years earlier, acquired their startup *for $19 billion.*

Moral of the story? Doing the opposite can work.

Other notable businesses that started during the Great Recession include:

- Groupon (2008)
- Uber (2009)

- Venmo (2009)
- Square (2009)
- Instagram (2010)
- Pinterest (2010)

WHAT IF CHANGE IS EASIER THAN YOU THINK?

The problem that many of us face when considering making a change is that it can sometimes seem too big, too overwhelming. Sure, "doing the opposite" might sound great in theory, but truly, how do you actually do that? Where do you start? That sort of change can seem very intimidating.

But what if it wasn't so tough after all? As it turns out, maybe it doesn't have to be.

I want you to picture in your mind a giant ocean tanker. Think about how massive they are—usually more than 1,000 feet long and weighing more than 50 tons. There is *a lot* of momentum keeping that tanker heading in a certain direction.

So how then does the captain of that giant ship change its direction? Most people think that the captain turns the wheel and the wheel turns the rudder. Simple, right? Wrong. In actuality, there is so much water pressure on the rudder that it is impossible to turn.

What happens instead is this: When the captain turns the wheel, the wheel turns a little mini-rudder called a "trim tab" that sits at the end of the actual rudder. The trim tab moves a bit, changing the water pressure around the real rudder, and that is what allows the bigger rudder to move. Only then does the massive ship begin to change course and head in a new direction.

It is the little change that makes the big change happen.

This actually is how a lot of change occurs in the world, whether we are talking about a ship, or a ship of state, or a basketball team, or a person. Little changes are often the fulcrum that fosters bigger ones.

Say What, Coach?

Probably the most successful college coach in any sport ever was basketball coach John Wooden of my alma mater UCLA, (Go Bruins!) At one time, Wooden's teams

- Won an astonishing 88 games in a row, and
- 10 championships in 12 years

Wooden himself was named Coach of the Year a record seven times, and he was the first person ever to be enshrined in the Basketball Hall of Fame as both a player and a coach. In 2003, President George W. Bush awarded the coach the highest civilian honor a person can get, the Presidential Medal of Freedom.

But John Wooden's legacy is about a lot more than beautiful basketball and a lot of championships. What the coach was really committed to was success in life; he knew that how you play the game of basketball was how you played the game of life. That bigger lesson was his true mission.

In fact, so committed was he to teaching life skills and success strategies that Coach Wooden spent 14 years creating what would eventually be known as his "Pyramid of Success." *Success* magazine, among many others, was so impressed with the pyramid's wisdom and applicability that it created an online course devoted to it dubbed "The Wooden Effect." With articles, videos, and quizzes, The Wooden Effect aims to impart the great coach's lessons. You too can learn how to "make each day your masterpiece" by going to https://www.thewoodeneffect.com.

John Wooden knew a few things about success. One of the things he knew was that little things matter; that counterintuitively, to win big you need to start small. A famous example is that when a blue-chip freshman player got to UCLA (or any player for that matter), the very first thing that happened on the very first day of practice is that he was taught . . . how to tie his shoes.

Of course players knew how to tie their sneakers, but the wise old coach knew something they did not. He knew that maybe, just maybe, they had gotten sloppy over the years, and that sturdy shoes and ankles were key to success in their sport.

But the lesson was a lot bigger than that. Coach Wooden also knew and often said, "It's the little details that matter. Little things make big things happen." Wooden was a stickler for fundamentals, and he believed that by relearning how to tie their shoes correctly, he was setting the context for his players to do everything correctly.

> *Coach Wooden called all the freshmen together and walked us into the locker room. We sat there like dutiful sponges ready to soak it all up, knowing that he was about to give us the key to heaven on earth, show us the path, guide us to become the next great team in history.*
>
> *His first words were, "Men, this is how you put your shoes and socks on."*
>
> *We were stunned. We looked around and at each other. Are you kidding me? We're all high school All-America players and here is this silly little old man showing us how to put on our shoes and socks!*
>
> *Over the course of time, he also showed us how to tuck in our shirts and tie the proper knot on the drawstring of our game shorts, how to shower and properly dry ourselves, how we would practice and prepare for games, and also how we should study for our classes. He showed us how to conduct our lives.*
>
> —**Bill Walton,** from his autobiography,
> *Back from the Dead*

Analysis Paralysis

Yes, change can seem scary. People sometimes fall into what is known as "analysis paralysis," trying to figure what needs to happen when, by who, how, and so on and so on and so on. Not infrequently, as a result, nothing happens.

But what if booming your business wasn't so hard after all? What if Coach Wooden was right and it really is true that it is the little changes that make the big things happen? In that case, just a small change in the right place can send your business in a new, better, more productive, more profitable, positive direction.

So, the good news is that you do not need to rethink your entire enterprise to take things to the next level. You do not have to overthink it. Making a change and getting the results you want can be a little trim tab adjustment away.

BOOM YOUR BUSINESS BOTTOM LINE

▶ It might seem odd to hear that what works is to think like George Costanza, but in this context, it does. The key is to do the opposite of those who do nothing. Opportunity awaits those who realize that the conventional wisdom is often wrong.

▶ Similarly, Coach John Wooden knew a thing or two about success, and it behooves us to recall his wise words: Little changes make big things happen.

▶ Warren Buffett had it right too: When opportunity presents itself, reach for a bucket, not a thimble. Such is the case now. You are ready for a new direction—after all, you are reading this book. That alone equals opportunity. Grab your bucket and think BIG.

▶ And finally, realize that your job is to act like the captain of a great ship, knowing that all it takes is a small trim tab tweak to produce a new direction. What does that mean for you? Look at key areas in your business and consider where a small tweak in the exact right spot can yield a new direction and a big shift. Be a trim tab.

CHAPTER 3

MONEY WHILE YOU SLEEP

Your past does not equal your future.
—Tony Robbins

You have to admit, grinding is all the rage these days. Gotta grind. Grind it out. Grind or die. "Someone busier than you is grinding right now." Maximize your productivity. Hustle! Create that side hustle. Turn it into your main hustle. Do the hustle!

The modern mandate to grind-or-die is like being a hamster on a wheel, and I dare you to show me a smart, happy hamster. The hamster's work life goes like this: get on the wheel, get to work, start spinning, don't look back, don't slow down, don't dare rest, just keep spinning out toward some goal that will never be reached because one either becomes addicted to the grind or burns out from exhaustion.

There has got to be a better way, right?

There is in fact a different and better way to work that will allow you to boom your business or career and make more money without killing yourself. If you are a small business person who is working 80-hour weeks, I am talking to you. If you are a freelancer who doesn't turn down any project, no matter how time-consuming or horrible the client, I'm looking at you.

The secret is to not work harder, but smarter, and to make money while you sleep.

Note that I am not suggesting, and nor would you want to hear, that hard work is a bad idea. The old adage that success is 1 percent inspiration and 99 percent perspiration is true. Working hard in and on your business is good.

But the hard work that can propel a business or career or endeavor forward is different—much different—than the grind-it-out-at-all-costs, hamster-on-a-wheel ethos that camouflages as hard work these days. The trick is to work hard *when you want to or need to*, but also to have as much time away as you need to have while still growing your business.

In his great book, *The 4-Hour Workweek*, Timothy Ferriss shares how he went from working 80 hours a week and making $40,000 a year to working 4 hours a week and making $40,000 a month. Quite the trick, right? Yet it wasn't a trick at all, it was strategic. Ferriss figured out an easier, better, more lucrative way to work, and in the process, he created a blueprint: work smarter, work less, generate passive income.

Working Smarter, Not Harder, in Action

Frederick Taylor was an industrial engineer who worked for Bethlehem Steel at the turn of the twentieth century. Tasked with increasing productivity at the plant (a common desire in the early Industrial Revolution), Taylor made a fascinating discovery: *He was able to increase the productivity of workers at the factory fourfold*, not by making them work more, but merely by enlarging the width of their shovels.

Example:[1] Ben Dechesare graduated from Stanford and became an investment banker, a demanding, all-consuming profession if ever there was one. He started working incredibly long hours, and it came to a head at 3 a.m. one morning while he was driving home. "Having pulled four to five all-nighters previously, [I] crashed into a tree on the side of the road." Not surprisingly, after waking up in the emergency room, Dechesare decided to take stock and reevaluate his life and decisions.

Clearly needing to revamp things, but unwilling to simply chuck it all without a plan, Dechesare began with a simple side hustle—a blog related to working in the mergers and acquisitions market. It caught on, and before long, potential consulting and coaching clients began to contact him. No one was more surprised than Dechesare when he was soon making as much with his new side hustle as he was with his "real job," while working "a fraction of the time."

Being no dummy, he began to create and sell more products from his newly popular blog, which allowed him "to travel to Hawaii and Aruba to go snorkeling, surfing, and shark-cage diving."

Eventually, Dechesare says, he was able to free up "a ton" more time, double his revenues, and put "the majority of my income on autopilot. If I didn't do any further work from that point on, I would still make two to three times my previous monthly income simply by writing for my site (4 to 5 hours a week), and doing limited consulting (10 hours). You could say that I increased my income almost three times while reducing my hours (by six to nine times.)"

Not bad, eh?

Ferriss says that in his case, he got down to working only four hours a week (although if you follow his popular blog or listen to his equally popular podcast at Tim.blog, you would be forgiven if you think, as I do, that he works quite a bit more than four hours a week).

Needless to say, of course you can work more than just four hours a week, but you could also work less than you do now *while making more*. Especially in this economy, after everything we have all been through, being smart about your precious time is essential.

Getting from here to there is a three-step process.

STEP 1: ENGAGE IN AN 80-20 ANALYSIS

As you may know, the 80-20 rule, generally speaking, states that 80 percent of your income comes from 20 percent of your customers, but the idea is actually a bit more complicated—and interesting and useful—than that.

The 80-20 rule was coined in the 1900s by an Italian economist named Vilfredo Pareto (which is why the 80-20 rule is also sometimes called Pareto's Principle), who realized that 80 percent of the wealth and income in Italy was owned by 20 percent of the population. But Pareto didn't stop there. He also observed that 80 percent of the peas in his garden were produced by 20 percent of his plants. Indeed, he found this principle to be generally applicable in many cases, with the upshot being that 80 percent of someone's results often stem from 20 percent of their efforts.

Since then, various people have taken Pareto's Principle and applied it to different scenarios. For example, 80 percent of your complaints might come from 20 percent of your customers, or 80 percent of your website traffic could come from 20 percent of your pages. Maybe 80 percent of your income comes from 20 percent of your work.

Abby is a hairstylist. Learning of the 80-20 rule, she did an analysis in order to discover where most of her new clients originated. She did not expect to discover that that at least 80 percent came from referrals from her existing clients. Abby thereafter completely stopped her Facebook ad campaign and instead created a word-of-mouth marketing plan, offering discounts and loyalty rewards to current customers who referred people to her.

Or what about Harvard graduate student Carla? The semester assignment in her digital communications class was to create a blog and monitor its success. At the halfway point of the class, the professor evaluated all of the blogs. Though well written, Carla's blog ranked dead last in terms of traffic.

Carla knew of the 80-20 rule and decided to apply it to her assignment. Her blunt evaluation was that while she spent a vast majority of her time writing great sentences, it was for naught because no one ever read them. So she analyzed her blog traffic with a few key questions in mind:

- Which 20 percent of her links generated 80 percent of her traffic? (She would market to them more.)
- Who were her core, top 20 percent readers? (She started writing for them more.)
- Which blogs and topics were her best performers? (She would write more about those topics.)

As a result of her analysis, Carla understood her best performing blogs better, and understood her top 20 percent of readers better. She then redesigned her site to match that audience more closely and began to focus her content on her most popular topics. By the end of the semester, Carla had grown her site traffic by more than 220 percent.[2]

As you begin to evaluate your business and implement the 80-20 rule for yourself, start by taking a hard look at what you do, how you spend your time, who your customers are, and so on. Which 20 percent of your customers, and what type of customers, make you the most money? What do the best have in common? What about the worst? What 20 percent of your products generate 80 percent of your income? Which 20 percent of your website pages get the most clicks? Which 20 percent of your employees make you the most money?

But then what? If you are going to begin to concentrate your efforts on those things that get you the best results, how will all of the other stuff get done?

STEP 2: GET THE HELP YOU NEED

When you run a business, whether it is a one-person shop or something much bigger, it is nevertheless still probably safe to say that you are too busy. And that's understandable; it's your nature. An entrepreneur is many things—smart, ambitious, hardworking, confident, and driven. But it is those very traits that get us into trouble. Because you are so smart and capable, you may think you need to do it all yourself, or that you can do it all yourself, or that if you want a job done right, you have to do it yourself.

Wrong, wrong, and wrong.

I once had a great therapist who helped me work through some issues at a time when I really needed a great therapist to help me work through some issues. One of the best tricks he used was to tell me, "Steve, that's a thinking error."

Let's say we were talking about my weight, and let's say I said something like, "I just don't have time to work out." Dino would politely say, "Steve, that's a thinking error." A thinking error was a story I would tell myself to justify inaction or the wrong action. Of course, it was not true that I did not have time to work out. I was just too lazy or unmotivated, or both. But once I saw and admitted that was a thinking error, I was able to correct it (or at least better able!)

Entrepreneurs have their own thinking errors. They might say, for instance, that even if they are too busy, they *simply have to do it all themselves* because they can't afford to get help, or they can't find good help, or they don't have time to train someone.

And to that we say, "Thinking error!"

If this sounds like you and you want to grow your business, one of the very first changes you will have to make is to correct this thinking error. The fact is, you can't afford not to get the help you need.

Getting help serves two purposes. First, it frees you up to do the 20 percent of things that you *should be doing* with your time, those things that give you the best results and that, it is safe to say, are likely the things you like and are best at.

Maybe what you learned in your 80-20 analysis is that you are great at sales and that they generate the vast majority of your income but that operations, which is *not* your strong suit, consumes most of your time. What you should not be doing then is ordering supplies or creating timesheets or managing payroll, etc. But you will only be able to make more money and have more fun by concentrating on sales *if you hire someone else to handle all of the other details.*

So, how do you get the help you need? There are options.

Hire (More) Staff

This is obviously obvious, but maybe not. For instance, maybe you think that hiring an office manager is cost-prohibitive.

Thinking error.

Hiring the help you need doesn't cost, it pays. You just have to make the commitment.

> *Until one is committed, there is hesitancy, the chance to draw back, always ineffectiveness. Concerning all acts of initiative (and creation) there is one elementary truth, the ignorance of which kills countless ideas and splendid plans:*
>
> *The moment one definitely commits oneself, then Providence moves too.*
>
> *All sorts of things occur to help one that would never otherwise have occurred. A whole stream of events issues from the decision, raising in one's favor all manner of unforeseen incidents and meetings and material assistance, which no man could have dreamed would have come his way.*
>
> *I have learned a deep respect for one of Goethe's couplets:* **"Whatever you can do, or dream you can, begin it. Boldness has genius, power, and magic in it."**
>
> **—W. H. Murray,** *The Scottish Himalayan Expedition*

If you take bold action, if you actually commit to not only doing the 80-20 exercise, but following through on what you learn, the result will be that you will be far more effective, will spend far less time on the things that bore you, and *you are going to make more money.* But this only happens if you free yourself by getting extra help. The rule is this:

> *Take the risk then make the money, not make the money then take the risk.*

Yes, that might seem backwards, but it is not. Every great business is a division of labor, and the very best allow, nay insist, that those involved do what they are best at. *That* is how you take it to the next level.

You could look at it this way: if you don't have an assistant, you *are* an assistant.

Outsource

One of the easiest and most affordable ways to free up your time is to outsource the mundane and the not-so-mundane to a virtual assistant (VA).

The vast array of things that a VA can do is simply amazing:

- Handling email
- Setting appointments and meetings
- Database management
- Website development and maintenance
- Social media posting and monitoring
- Writing, proofreading, and editing
- Invoicing
- Marketing research, legal research, any research
- PowerPoint preparation

VAs can be found in the United States, of course, but more inexpensively overseas. While their prices are competitive and enticing, one thing to be aware of is the possibility of communication issues. Working with people in different time zones and for whom English is not their first language can sometimes be vexing. So, keep that in mind.

Other Options

"Working smarter, not harder" is an exercise in creativity. To succeed at this requires that you loosen your moorings, release control, and think anew. As such, getting the help you need can also be done creatively. Options abound:

Hire someone part-time. Hiring part-time or seasonal help is a fine way to (1) learn how to delegate, and (2) get affordable help.

Hire an independent contractor. We are in, after all, the gig economy.

Hire an intern. Interns are affordable, usually quite enthusiastic, and almost always ready to take on any sort of project.

One useful resource is StudentOpportunityCenter.com, which connects companies with MBA students at 400-plus US universities like Yale, NYU, Rice, and the University of Texas. The classes these students take require them to complete some form of "project-based learning," where they have to contribute real value to real companies. You can go to this site and get free help from the best and the brightest. See? Options abound!

STEP 3: MAKE MONEY
WHILE YOU SLEEP

You already run a business that has traditionally kept you quite busy. The last thing you need is a new profit center that is time-consuming or labor-intensive. Rather, what you need and deserve are profit centers that generate passive income; profit centers that put at least part of your income on autopilot.

An e-commerce website is the obvious example of this step in action. With a physical, traditional store that you own and run, you need to be there most of the time. When the store closes for the day, so too does your ability to make money. Not so e-commerce. With a good e-commerce site, your selling and sales are automatic, generating income any time of the day, 24/7, from anywhere in the world.

And because e-commerce is but one option, imagine waking up one morning to discover an alert on your phone from Shopify, telling you that your e-commerce store generated more than a grand last night. Or maybe you get an email telling you that your stock dividend doubled. What about a call from a colleague, informing you that that organic frozen pizza startup you invested in scored a deal with Whole Foods and is going to be in 500 stores nationwide? Pretty sweet, that's what.

> I remember saying to my mentor, "If I had more money, I would
> have a better plan." He quickly responded, "I would suggest
> that if you had a better plan, you would have more money." You
> see, it's not the amount that counts, it's the plan that counts.
> **—Jim Rohn**

As you think through what your new passive-income profit centers could be, you should follow three ground rules:

1. Ideally, the new business/profit center should be one that you can test small, without a lot of risk, to see if it works.
2. It should be something that can generate income consistently.
3. And finally, it needs to be something that can mostly be run without your day-to-day involvement, that really does generate money while you sleep.

Brainstorm and Test

For many years, Amazon only sold books, and to most of us, that alone seemed incredible. Jeff Bezos realized that being able to sell books online in a virtual bookstore was revolutionary because actual physical bookstores (which were his competition when he launched Amazon in the late nineties) could only house several thousand books at most. In contrast, Bezos's online store could sell any book in print, and to anywhere in the world.

For you and me and most people on the planet, creating "Earth's Biggest Bookstore," as Amazon was originally billed, would have been enough. But not for Bezos. He had set his sights on something much bigger, the fruit of which we see today. Earth's biggest bookstore was merely a test for Earth's Biggest Store.

Jeff Bezos and the crew at Amazon were using the bookstore model to see what worked, to see how to conduct e-commerce (because no one had ever done it before), and to see how selling books could be a template for selling much more.

And that, ladies and gentlemen, is why Jeff Bezos is the richest man in the world.

That said, one thing I always advise small business people is that there is no need to reinvent the wheel. Big businesses have scores of brilliant MBAs generating creative ideas that we can emulate. Great entrepreneurs like Bezos have already figured out things that would take us years, if ever, to duplicate. Instead of inventing something new, look at ideas big businesses have perfected and emulate them. In this case, Amazon tested the idea of e-commerce before becoming the everything store.

And you can, too. Testing small to see what works is smart. Start by brainstorming money-while-you-sleep ideas and test them out.

You could, for example:

- Start a YouTube channel, generating ad revenue.
- Create an online course with prerecorded videos and lessons.
- Launch an e-commerce business on Amazon, eBay, Etsy, or your own site.
- Write and sell an e-book.
- Buy rental property.
- Create a drop-shipping business.

- Airbnb part of your property.
- Become an angel investor.
- License your content or other intellectual property.
- Buy a laundromat, vending machines, or ATMs.
- Buy a franchise.

Make Sure It Really Is Passive, Repeatable, and Automatic

As you brainstorm ideas to test, remember that what you are looking for are options that can generate consistent revenue without you having to do much after the initial setup.

Of course, there will be *something* to do, but it should be qualitatively and quantitatively different from the business you now run. Most entrepreneurs start businesses that they operate daily, not ones that run themselves. This is not that. This will be different, better. A great new passive-income-generating idea (or two or three!) can revolutionize your work world. Between that and spending your time on your top 20 percent most productive activities, your work life can be transformed.

But remember, it all starts with this thought: "Whatever you can do, or dream you can, begin it. Boldness has genius, power, and magic in it."

Be *bold*, my friend!

BOOM YOUR BUSINESS BOTTOM LINE

▶ Creating passive income, a.k.a money while you sleep, is the key to working smarter, not harder. Doing so is a three-step process.

▶ The first step requires a hard look at your business and figuring out what you sell, and do, that brings you the most profit and joy. Traditionally, this is called an 80-20 analysis.

▶ The second step requires that you delegate some of your minutia work to an assistant (virtual or otherwise) or some other employee or contractor who can pick up the slack and help you free up some time. If you do not have an assistant, you are an assistant.

▶ The last step is to create some affordable passive-income streams.

CHAPTER 4

GET BIGGER CLIENTS

Your playing small does not serve the world.
—Nelson Mandela

People I know, clients of mine, readers of my columns and books, and attendees of my speeches, seminars, and webinars have all used the various strategies I am outlining in this book to great success. But of them all, the strategy in this chapter—getting bigger clients—easily has had the biggest effect on my own personal life and business.

The ideas I am outlining in this chapter literally quadrupled my income in under two years.

Here's what happened: A long time ago, in a galaxy far, far away, I was an unhappy lawyer. I liked the law, and certainly always gave 100 percent to my clients, but suing people was just too adversarial a life for me. So, even though I had recently published my first books (the *Ask a Lawyer* series), and even though this, my very first business—the Strauss Law Firm—was a success, and even though I was a professional making a good living, I was actually pretty miserable.

It turned out that I liked the small business part of running my law firm more than the law part. Given that I come from a family of small business people and entrepreneurs, maybe it was not surprising that I enjoyed finding and getting clients more than I did finding and suing defendants.

So when *USA TODAY* came knocking, asking me if I would be interested in being the "online small business columnist" for their new website, USATODAY.com (literally, I was the second online columnist they ever hired), I jumped at the chance, even if I had but a vague notion of what an "online columnist" was at the time, the internet being so new and all.

But soon I figured it out and was able to parlay that great opportunity into a nice little gig creating and selling content, happy to leave the law behind.

But the operative word in that last sentence is "little."

The issue I had to solve in that new business was this: Who buys small business content? My initial answer was sell to chambers of commerce and other nonprofits that worked to assist small business people.

But the problem with selling to nonprofits was that they had no profit.

I could—and did—get chambers to pay me, say, $100 a month for my content, but even if I lined up 25 chambers (which was no small sales feat), that was still only a paltry $2,500 a month. Even with extra income from other projects, I was not earning what I was worth.

But then life changed, radically and for the better.

For a few months I had been chasing my first corporate client, Microsoft. The company had previously written me, suggesting a topic for a *USA TODAY* column, and I used the intro as an opportunity to continue speaking with them about ways we might be able to team up. I really didn't know what I was doing or how to pitch them, but that didn't stop me.

Fast-forward a few months, and I was in Paris with my wife. We had scrimped and saved, and it was her birthday and we were atop the Eiffel Tower one night when I got a phone call from back in the States. Was I interested in being the columnist for a new small business site Microsoft was creating? The offer they made that night for one ongoing monthly corporate gig was more than I made each month from all of those 25 nonprofits combined.

Needless to say, the light that went on over my head at that moment was almost as bright as those illuminating the rest of the City of Lights, or, as a pal of mine who was a lawyer at Microsoft put it to me later, "Once you feed from the corporate trough, you will never want to go back."

What I soon realized was that I had been thinking far too small. If I wanted the big bucks, I needed to think bigger and target bigger clients. So that's what I did, and that's what I do.

With this strategy, I more than quadrupled my income in about two years by pivoting, targeting, pitching, connecting with, and soon, working for some of the biggest companies and brands in the world: Microsoft, Bank of America, Visa, the US State Department, and many more.

You can too.

What one person can do, another can do.

GETTING BIG MONEY CLIENTS

There are a lot of ways to target bigger clients that have bigger budgets. A friend of mine who is a real estate agent in Los Angeles did it very successfully, but under much more dire circumstances than my own. His story is illustrative.

The year was 2007, and my pal was selling single-family homes throughout the southland. He made a decent living, but it was a heck of a lot of work: driving over 100 miles a day, multiple showings, deals falling through, cranky clients.

And that was *before* the Not-So-Great Recession.

Then the economy fell off the cliff due to the bursting of the housing bubble and his entire livelihood was suddenly at risk. Almost overnight, my friend's portfolio of deals dwindled to a paltry few. Scared and not knowing what to do or where to turn, he went to see a family friend who was an old real estate broker. He was given this advice:

"I'm going to tell you the secret," the friend said. "You can do little deals, or you can do big deals. You can have little clients, or you can have big clients. You can stick with selling single-family homes, or you can sell apartment houses and commercial real estate. And here's the thing: If you switch to selling bigger properties for bigger clients, you will not only make a whole lot more money, but basically, you will be doing so for about same amount of work."

In a few short sentences, my pal was given the keys to the kingdom.

Given that he really had very few other options, and that the idea of actually growing his business in the middle of what was then the worst recession in 50 years, my pal decided he had little to lose and a lot to gain, so he would reinvent his real estate business. He began by taking classes on commercial real estate. He sought out commercial real estate brokers, took them to lunch, and picked their brains. He also hired a virtual assistant who specialized in marketing. Finally, he rebranded himself as a high-end commercial real estate broker.

Over the next 12 months, even though the real estate market in the United States generally, and Los Angeles specifically, tanked, and even though my pal was able to close only three deals that whole year, he made more money in those three deals than he had with all of the single-family home sales he had closed only two years prior.

These days, he routinely makes seven figures selling high-end commercial properties.

What Is a Big Money Client or Customer?

Before we dive more specifically into how to land a big money client, it's important to define exactly what we mean when we use that term. A big money client or customer is a person, a company, or an organization that has a significant budget (i.e., *enough to pay you what you are really worth*). They have the revenue, processes, budgets, foresight, and capacity to hire and pay individuals and companies significantly more than, say, what a small business or nonprofit could pay or would pay or what a "regular" individual would want to pay.

Bottom line: Big money clients are major corporations, governments, and high-net-worth individuals.

There are many benefits of getting bigger clients and customers:

More money. Bigger clients pay more. Period.

Repeat business. You are more likely going to get repeat business because big money and corporate clients like doing business with people they know, and they are loyal.

You will get more and better referrals. When big-budget clients like your work, there is a greater likelihood of them referring other big-budget clients to you.

You will have the ability to charge more. Once you gain a reputation as someone who is able to handle these sorts of clients, your brand and buzz build, and as a result, you will be considered more top-tier and therefore able to charge more.

You will build your brand. A cousin to the benefit above is that your brand will transform into something bigger, better, and more desirable. Creating content for Microsoft is a lot different, and more impressive, than creating content for the Greater Tehachapi Chamber of Commerce.

You will get bigger deals. Once you become a big deal, you will get big deals.

And finally, you're going to create a business that can scale. We will dig into this next, but if you are able to get and handle bigger clients, you will necessarily be scaling your business because you will need help managing the extra workload.

Be Prepared to Produce

You need to understand that these clients are different than other clients.

First, they pay the big bucks for a reason—they expect big results.

Second, they tend to be slow. One of the beautiful things about small businesses is that we are flexible; we can pivot quickly and make decisions rapidly. Big companies don't do that, literally can't do that. Decisions especially tend to come down the pike slowly, and there are usually many stakeholders in the process. So you have to be prepared to be patient and deal with different constituencies.

Finally, you have to do great work. Quality, quality, quality. You have to be worthy of the trust that they are going to put into you. But if you do produce, if you do great work, you are going to be commensurately recompensed.

So OK, all of this begs the question: How do you find and get these demanding, rewarding, high-paying clients?

There are two ways to get higher paying clients:

1. You find them, or
2. They find you

Now, of these two, most of us go with the first strategy, which is, you find them. That's great, and it works. But better, in my opinion and experience, is if they find you. And in the next chapter I am going to share several strategies about how to do just that— how to position yourself, your business, and your brand in such a way that these big money, high-paying corporate and government clients, and high-net-worth individuals, will not only want to work with you, they will actively seek you out. That is what started happening with me once I started doing this.

But before you get there, you will need to find them.

FINDING HIGH-PAYING CLIENTS

There are three main ways to go out and find high-paying clients: (1) prospecting, (2) supplier diversity programs, and (3) social media.

Let's note up front that prospecting is not a "get-rich-quick" scheme, it is a "get-rich-slow" scheme. That said, when I say slow, we are not talking about years, we are likely talking about less than a year but more than a few months. So although I am not suggesting that you will get your first big contract in two months, you could get it in six months. While that first contract will not make you rich, once you start doing this again and again, and as you start to get repeat business and more contracts, your business will scale and it can really change your life.

Small business boom here we come!

20 years ago, two young illustrators moved to Los Angeles with the dream of starting their own animation company. Being new to town, they decided to open up shop in trendy Santa Monica. The problem was that the big movie and animation studios are not located near Santa Monica; most are a good half hour away, and Disney, the king of animation, was over in the valley, an hour away.

The two partners soon realized their mistake, especially as they had targeted Disney from the get-go as their best bet for a big client. They knew that to land this client, they needed to meet Disney execs, so what did they do? They admitted their mistake, got out of their lease, and moved their little shop over the hill to Burbank.

And then they specifically made an effort to go out to lunch every day in the area, to attend local industry meetings and workshops, and to go to mixers, all with the intent of meeting Disney executives.

They did. It worked. To this day, Disney is still their biggest client.

PROSPECTING

There are several steps that go into prospecting for bigger clients and customers.

Step 1: Think Blue Sky

Begin by making a list of companies that you would like to do business with, companies that you think likely would buy your services. Think big. Come up with a list of obvious contenders, companies in your area, and businesses that fit your profile, but also consider dream clients—the Disneys of your world.

Beyond just your own list of companies that you know, you need to expand your list to include businesses beyond your knowledge. Research. Read. Google. Watch corporate videos. Look at industry news and publications. Expand your list.

Then look at what your competitors are doing and with whom. No, of course you do not want to steal their business, but what they do and with whom is important to know. Think about similar companies that you could work with.

The idea here is to make a list of likely candidates that you could do business with. Start with 10, maybe 20. Think of this as a funnel; this list of potential suitors would be at the top of your funnel.

Once you have your list, you need to learn more about these companies. What is their corporate culture? How much do they contract with small businesses? Where do they advertise, and who are their clients? You need to get a sense of the vibe of these companies because if you are going to pitch them, you will need to be able to speak their language.

Step 2: Find Decision Makers Within the Company

You will need to find the right people within each company who will have the interest and budget to hire your firm. This is often where people stumble or get stuck, but truly, it is not as difficult as it sounds.

Finding the right person or people requires research, tenaciousness, charm, bravado, and resourcefulness. It is a matter of thinking creatively and being willing to put yourself out there. Here's where to look to find the right people within that big company:

1. **Their website.** Go to their site and look at the company's structure and divisions. Which fit your business?
2. **Annual reports.** Public companies publish annual reports that are a wealth of information if you are willing to dig into the minutiae.
3. **Google.** Google and read as much about the company as you can. Options and/or titles of people that you had not considered will likely pop up.
4. **Social media, especially LinkedIn.** Social media generally, and LinkedIn specifically, is a treasure trove of corporate content. LinkedIn has a great search function that allows you to search for people by title, company, interests, duties, you name it.
5. **Titles.** Obvious titles of people you may look for would be VP of your division, human resources, buyers, purchasing managers or agents, sales director, sales reps, and procurement officers or managers.

The idea at this stage is to create a large list of potential people to prospect. Once you have a rough idea of whom to pitch, I suggest picking up the phone and simply calling the company's main number and asking for that person. In all likelihood, you will not reach him or her but instead, be sent to an assistant. Good, go with it.

Put a smile on your face (people can hear it through the phone), get your charm on, and ask for help. Explain to the person who you are and why you are calling. Ask for their help—Is Ms. X the right person you should be calling? Is there someone else she can suggest with whom you should speak? Could she recommend managers or directors in other divisions who might need your services?

The point at this stage is simply to compile a big list of potential suitors.

Another way to do that is simply to ask around. People want to help, they like to help, but they do not know you need help unless you ask. So ask. Let your network know that you are looking for a contact withing a certain company. You just may get a lead that can make all the difference.

Step 3: First Contact

You are not looking to sell at this stage. Instead, the whole purpose at this juncture is just to introduce yourself, make a great first impression, and narrow down your list.

Needless to say, these days there is no shortage of ways to get in contact with people—calling, texting, email, social media—all are options. For our purposes, however, some are definitely better than others. A process that works is this:

1. Physical Mailing

How many emails do you get a day? And how many do you delete? Exactly. That is why you don't want to start with an email; it is simply too easy to have it get buried in the inbox, ignored, or deleted.

Instead, consider sending something by snail mail.

The second chapter of this book is entitled "Do the Opposite." The opposite often works because it gets you noticed. That is definitely the case here. Put together a nice, tight, introductory letter and then—and this is key—make your letter or package "chunky." Maybe you have a doodad, or a key chain, or a pen. Whatever it is, add it to your envelope.

Then—and this is also key—hand address the envelope and mail it. The prospect will receive a handwritten envelope/package with something chunky obviously inside. Can't delete that! How likely is that person to open that envelope? Very. Your prospect gets hundreds of emails a week, but if you follow this process, he or she will undoubtedly open, read, and remember your chunky envelope above the rest.

Marketing gold.

One last tip: Make sure that you add a P.S. to the bottom of your letter. Why? I don't know why it is, but I do know that, for some reason, even if they don't read the whole letter, people almost always read the P.S. So make yours snappy and memorable.

What Doesn't Work

- What doesn't work is to start your letter without using the person's name, for example, "Dear marketing manager."
- What doesn't work is to write a dense, 10-paragraph letter.
- What doesn't work is to send a generic letter.
- What doesn't work is to have typos in your letter.

The point of this process is to make a connection with somebody. You need to pitch yourself, and your business, and do it quickly and in a way that is both professional and clever. The whole idea here is to find the right company, and the right person, and to start a conversation with that person to forge a connection.

Eventually, what you are really looking for is someone who will become a champion for your business within the company.

2. Zoom or Phone Call

There was a time, pre-COVID-19, where I would say that at this point in the process you should look toward trying to set up an in-person meeting, but these days, Zoom is almost as good. You need to make a connection, correct? While in-person is still best, Skype, Zoom, or FaceTime can work just about as well. Either way, the question people are going to be asking themselves as you pitch them is "What's in it for me?"

The main purpose then of your first contact is to introduce yourself and your company. But it needs to go deeper than that. What you are really trying to do is begin a conversation. What are their needs? What do you have in common? The real question you have to get answered is: What issue of theirs can you take off their plate?

3. Proposal

Once you have your prospects' attention, it is time to show them exactly how you can help, make their life easier, make their business better, make their customers happier, build their brand, solve some problem they have—any and all of the above.

You do this by sending them a proposal. Your proposal may take the form of a Word document or a PowerPoint presentation. Maybe you will make a video. Whatever the case and whatever the form, the elements of any great proposal must contain at least this:

- Who you are and what you have done; why you should be taken seriously
- How your business is unique, different, better
- How what you do solves their problem
- Who else believes in you

However you do it, keep in mind that your job is not to sell, it is to help. If prospects get that you are there to help them, they are going to be far more receptive to what you have to say.

Whether they need cleaning services or a new animator, if you can make this person's life easier, if you can help the company solve a problem, if you are cheaper or better or more convenient or easier to work with or offer better services, then they are going to want to hire you.

SUPPLIER DIVERSITY PROGRAMS

Almost all Fortune 500 companies have programs known as supplier diversity programs. These are programs in which the company makes a commitment to contract with small businesses owned by minorities, women, veterans, the disabled, and the LGBTQ+ community. There are approximately 16 different categories of businesses that fall into this "diverse" category. The bottom line is this: major corporations hire many different types of small businesses to supply them with a wide variety of needed goods and services, and these contracts are significant—six and seven figures significant.

Here's how to get started:

1. **Register with a certifying organization.** You need to be certified as a small/diverse business if you want a potential corporate client to bring you into its supplier diversity fold. There are many organizations that can certify your business is in fact at least 51 percent diversely owned:

   - The Small Business Administration
   - The National Minority Supplier Development Council
   - Vets First
   - The National Gay and Lesbian Chamber of Commerce
   - The United States Hispanic Chamber of Commerce
   - The National Women's Business Council

   There are many others too. Google it.

2. **Research supplier diversity events and sites.** There are both offline and online events that seek to match small businesses with corporations looking to contract with diverse small business suppliers. Offline, they are often called "business matchmaking" events.

   Online matchmaking occurs as well. For instance, the site Diversity411.com says, "Diversity411.com is an online matchmaking website designed to connect minority-owned and small vendors with large businesses that have immediate opportunities." The CVM blog is another good resource (https://blog.cvmsolutions.com).

If you specifically want to do business with the federal government (talk about a big money client!), here's a great tip: Register your business with the System for Award Management (SAM). SAM is an online database of companies seeking to work with federal agencies and, therefore, these agencies will search this database when looking for suppliers. You can register as a government contractor at https://federal.famr.us.

3. **Do your homework.** Supplier diversity is not charity; indeed there is a lot of competition for these lucrative contracts, so do your homework. Learn about supplier diversity programs generally, and the requirements of each company you are interested in working with in particular. Understand what a successful bid looks like, and speak with other small business owners who have had supplier diversity success.

4. **Target your market.** One of the great things about programs like these is that, unlike a prospecting endeavor where so much work necessarily goes into finding the exact right person to pitch, there is no need for that here. Instead, simply go to the company website, search for its supplier diversity program, and off you go.

These companies will have specific contracts that they need filled and specific requirements for the small businesses they are looking for to fill them. You will need to fill out many forms, create detailed proposals, woo the right people, and meet with the buyers.

SOCIAL MEDIA

Stone Melet had a great idea for a business.

A veteran of newsrooms before moving to San Francisco during the dot-com era and creating a successful startup that he later sold to eBay, Melet's latest idea tapped into his media background.

He decided that he would start to make "highlight books" for athletes—a package of press clippings, mementos, important documents, along with a video highlight reel, and more. Melet envisioned elegant, leather-clad books that family members could gift to the special athlete in their lives, or which the athletes themselves could buy to commemorate their careers.

The only question was, where would "BESTofLEGACY" begin to find clients? Social media. Melet started by going onto LinkedIn and targeting athletes in the Bay Area.

He searched for various local athletes who he thought might be interested in his product, and LinkedIn would show him which of his connections had some connection to those athletes. Melet would then kindly ask the person he knew for an introduction. Before long, BESTofLEGACY started getting big money professional athletes as clients.

Since then, Melet's business has thrived due to the many connections he has made with athletes and their spouses. The word-of-mouth for his products among that community is amazing.

But notably, it all started with a LinkedIn search.

And, maybe even more impressively, it was social media that allowed Melet to *grow his business* during the pandemic. Check it out—in his own words:

> *After the startup phase of the business, the number one key component to our success has been our direct and ongoing access to the athletes, and their spouses. When COVID hit we were in the middle of our annual Spring Training visits in Florida and Arizona. Typically around 28 of the 30 Major League Baseball teams invite us to spend a morning with their players.*

Roughly 3/4 of those visits were complete when the COVID plug was abruptly pulled. It was surreal. What would we do? What will become of our business if we were unable to continue to meet the players in person? And what about all the NBA, NFL, and NHL visits that were not going to now happen? We had just completed our best year ever—over 315 deals. We had no idea how we were going to keep the momentum going.

But at the end of the day, we still managed to close 300 deals in 2020, almost matching our previous year's record. How?

Instagram.

Prior to COVID, Instagram was merely a sideshow for our business. But necessity truly is the mother of invention. We encouraged every client to post about their book on Instagram. And then, every time an athlete/spouse/friend "liked" one of those posts, we had a new warm lead that we chased.

For the first time in over 15 years in business, we started closing deals with folks we'd never met in person, and in many cases, who had never actually seen a live BESTofLEGACY book. Instagram turned out to be a game changer for us.

Whether it is a major corporation that you are after, or a certain high-net-worth individual, social media makes it vastly easier to reach out to them. In fact, that is almost the easy part now because once you make that initial connection, you still have to go about landing that big fish the old-fashioned way: You have to impress and woo them.

BOOM YOUR BUSINESS BOTTOM LINE

▶ One of the best ways to boom your business is by targeting high-net-worth individuals, major corporations, and governments. They are the entities who have the budgets to pay big money fees. There are three main ways to find these sorts of clients.

▶ The first is good, old-fashioned prospecting. This is a matter of doing research and finding the right companies and people who would be interested in what you have to sell. You then reach out to them, creatively, and look to forge a relationship. If you can help them solve a problem, you are on your way.

▶ The second option is to tap into supplier diversity programs. Corporations have earmarked billions of dollars in contracts for certain minority small businesses. Getting your foot in the door in this world is a game changer.

▶ Finally, social media has made access easier than ever—if you take advantage of it!

CHAPTER 5

GETTING BIG CLIENTS TO FIND YOU

Brand yourself for the career you want,
not the job you have.
—**Dan Schawbel,** *New York Times*
bestselling author of *Promote Yourself*

Which person or company would you be more inclined to buy from or work with?

- Starbucks, or Joe's Coffee Shed?
- The Chicago Bulls, or the Albany Platoons?
- Richard Branson, or Maury Lapinski?

You get the point. Brands that people know have value (or at least perceived value). Generally speaking, when given a choice, most folks will choose to buy from a company that they have heard of over one they have not. Customers prefer brands. As such, if, instead of chasing work, you want work to chase you, it would behoove you to begin to think about your professional brand in this way.

In fact, whether you know it or not, and whether you like it or not, you and your business already have a brand, for good or ill. The problem for most small businesses is that they have a brand that comes by default, not design. And that is too bad because the power of a brand that pops is real.

BRANDTASTIC!

This idea of having a memorable, valuable reputation goes by different names. For a business, it's called branding. For an individual, it could be called branding, but it might also be called being an expert, or an influencer or thought leader. Yet it is all essentially the same thing: Your brand is your name, reputation, value, personality, expertise, differentiation, and promise, all rolled into one.

There are many reasons why building a personal brand behooves you:

Top of mind. A brand is memorable. When potential customers have a project that needs to get done, they will usually first think of a brand. Tht means, if you become well known in your field, they will think of you.

Credibility. When a person or business is in fact well known, people think that there must be a reason for that. You must be better, right?

Magnetism. A brand attracts people, projects, clients, money.

Money. Brands can, and usually do, charge more.

Opportunities. The better known you or your business becomes, the more people will hear of you, and the more people hear of you, the more they will want to work with you.

If you want to see the value of a great brand, consider Starbucks. The corporate behemoth began as a single store at Pike Place Market in Seattle. It became one of the world's most recognizable and valuable brands with roughly 20,000 stores worldwide because CEO Howard Schultz had a vision for something that was unique and better than the competition.

Prior to Starbucks, a coffee shop was just that—a coffee shop. But Schultz turned the pedestrian coffee shop into a destination meeting place: a cool spot with a great vibe where employees and customers alike are treated well, where music wafts in, where the coffee is spot-on, and where folks are willing to drop a five-spot for a caffe latte. Now that is a good brand!

> *Starbucks represents something*
> *beyond a cup of coffee.*
> **—Howard Schultz**

The point is this: People view well-known names and brands differently. They like them, want to work with them, and are willing to pay a premium to be associated with them. If your brand is doing its job, business will almost magically flock to you. Conversely, if yours is "meh," you are most certainly leaving money and opportunities on the table.

How then do you go about upping your branding game? It depends on the type of brand you want to elevate. If it is your own personal brand, then the trick is to become what is now known as a thought leader or an influencer.

A business brand is different and really is a matter of marketing and advertising (less sexy, yes, but no less effective). Throughout the remainder of this book, scores of strategies that can be applied to promoting your business brand are presented (specifically in Chapters 7, "Get One Million Hits," and 9, "The Digital Divide,") and so, for the sake of expediency and to avoid redundancy, we will leave that for those chapters and focus here on building your personal brand and thought leadership.

BECOMING AN INFLUENCER

While you need to become better known if you want to become an influencer, becoming an influencer is not simply about becoming better known. The two go hand in hand.

1. You need to do work that is worthy of being noticed, and then
2. You need to share that work in ways that get you noticed in your desired community.

Personal branding is about being well known for the right reasons. While Kim Kardashian can be "famous for being famous" (although truly, she is an incredible entrepreneur), we cannot, nor should we want that. Rather, becoming an influencer is about being excellent. It's about being different, unique, and better. It is about doing work that you believe in and that that sets you apart.

In the process of doing that great work, you will necessarily also strive to get the word out about who you are, what you do, why you do it, and why it is valuable. After all, a brand that no one hears about is not much of a brand, is it?

But if you do great work that resonates with people and serves the market, you *will* become better known, and that is the path we seek. As opposed to those people and businesses who either have a default blah brand or a trumped-up faux brand, being a real expert in your field will set you apart and get you the sort of meaningful, valuable, financially rewarding work that truly can take things to the next level.

A better brand will mean bigger deals with bigger clients for bigger bucks.

So, just how do you start to get known as one of the experts in your field, one who wields influence (hence, influencer), a name brand?

Be Very Specific

Finding your niche and really leaning into it sets you apart and makes you memorable. The value of that cannot be overstated. Having a specific brand is the way people will remember you. It is a hook they can hang their hat on.

There is simply so much noise out there now that getting heard, seen, and noticed above the din can be quite challenging. If you do not have a very specific topic and brand, it will be easy to get lost in the noise and never be noticed.

A great personal brand is unambiguous. People know what it stands for and what the person is all about. For example:

Bill Nye: The science guy, of course

Tony Robbins: Self-help guru

Billie Eilish: Incredible indie musician

Chip and Joanna Gaines: Remodeling duo extraordinaire

Ashton Kutcher: Hipster actor and entrepreneur

These are not wishy-washy personal brands. These are smart people who know who they are, what they do, why they are different and better, and they built their brands around those traits. Importantly, here, you also know what they *do not* do. Chip Gaines does not give financial advice. Billie Eilish is not a political commentator.

They know what their lane is, and they stay in it.

The same is true, by the way, for a great business brand. Think about Harley-Davidson for a moment. What is it you thought of when I mentioned that brand? Probably those distinctive hogs of a bike, maybe an outlaw image, that distinctive logo.

It's no mistake that that is what you thought of. Harley has spent a lot of money, time, and effort into burnishing that outlaw biker brand into our collective consciousness. But would you buy a Harley? I know I wouldn't. Aside from an aversion to motorcycles, the brand does not speak to me. But guess what? Harley-Davidson doesn't care. It is not trying to be all things to all people like, say, GE (a blah business brand if ever there was one). Instead, the marketing geniuses at Harley-Davidson know that a great brand attracts some people *and repels others*. It is the ones who love the brand that make them the money. It is a niche brand for a niche audience.

Grand brands know who their audience is. They know what they're good at, and they emphasize that. That's what Starbucks does. Nike and Disney, too. Those brands are not fuzzy; you know exactly who they are, what they stand for, what they sell, and what their corporate personality is. And that's what we must do too.

> *I like being in a rock and roll band, but I love being in a rock and roll brand.*
>
> **—Gene Simmons,** KISS

Your first step, therefore, in creating an influential personal brand is to decide what it is you want to stand for, what you want your brand to be. To be an influencer who breaks through, your brand must make sense, have integrity, and be true to who you are. You must be able to answer some essential questions such as: What are you great at? What are you committed to? What is it that you do that is unique, different, special, and better? And finally, what tools will best help you get the word out?

This process really works if yours is a service business, where you and the business are one in the same—professions like lawyers, doctors, writers, speakers, designers, creatives, and consultants. You become the work, the work becomes you, and your brand amplifies the whole. That is what works.

The Celebrity CEO

If anyone knows how to create a great, valuable personal brand from scratch, it is my friend Ramon Ray. In fact, Ramon wrote the book on it, called *The Celebrity CEO*.

Ramon began his career, some 20 plus years ago, working for the United Nations, but these days, he is a small business influencer and an in-demand speaker. So how did he get from there to here?

He did exactly what he recommends that we do in his book. The first thing you need to do, he says, once you know your focus, is to create a community. In his case, it was small business. That was his tribe. He strongly advises that you define that community narrowly too. "What you want," he says, "is to be a big fish in a small pond, not a small fish in a big pond," adding that, "by narrowing your target market, you will also be able to fine-tune your marketing and advertising messages. You will also know the market better, speak their language, and know the needs of that narrow market."

You then need to start creating content that speaks to that audience. "Content that they like will draw them to your brand," Ramon says. This is turn requires that you engage with your tribe—you don't just create content *for* them, you need to listen *to* them. "That is where social media comes into play. It is such a powerful tool for creating a community and building a brand. If you use it right, you will build up trust and name recognition. You can then offer your community products or solutions they want or need."

The key takeaway from Ramon is this: While a lot of entrepreneurs, or creatives, or solopreneurs are fine and have a fine business, you can really boom your brand by finding your niche, giving it your all, and showing your passion and commitment to your community. (You can learn more about Ramon at RamonRay.com.)

So that is the first step: You need to decide what it is that you love and what makes the most sense for you to commit to. What is your logical niche?

Is It Marketable?

Focus alone does not a brand make.

The trick is to come up with a personal brand that does two things simultaneously: Not only will it speak to your unique value, interests, and skills, but also, it needs to be something that resonates in the marketplace. This is not an academic exercise. Your intended brand has to play in the real world, it must be something that people and companies need and/or want:

- **A lawyer can brand herself as "The affordable attorney."**
  This works because it is unique, different, memorable,
  unexpected.
- **A dentist could become "The sedation dentist."** People
  generally don't like going to the dentist. So, while there are
  plenty of dentists that offer sedation dentistry, making it
  the hook would resonate with a specific (nervous) segment
  of the marketplace.
- **A comedian could become "The roastmaster general."**
  Sure, there are plenty of comedians out there, but only
  Jeffrey Ross figured out that becoming the one who best
  roasts people could be a ticket to being a name-brand
  comedian.

So this is the plan:

Step 1: Pick out that thing that can or does set you apart.

Step 2: Let the world know about it.

GETTING THE WORD OUT

Once you have decided upon a direction for your personal brand,
the next step is essential: You need to get the word out. Your community needs to learn that you are out there, and that you have a
unique and valuable take, and, as such, that you can and should be
looked upon as a thought leader in your field.

There are four ways to do that, and you need to engage in
all four:

1. By producing thought leadership content
2. By appearing in the media
3. By having a significant social media presence
4. By being unique and memorable

Let's drill down into each.

Create Thought Leadership Content

To be considered an expert in your field you need to produce content that speaks to that expertise. Once upon a time, that was much more difficult. You needed an editor or a producer to either publish your work or put you on the air. But today, most gatekeepers have been eliminated. If you want to share your expertise, there is nothing stopping you. Aside from (obviously) having a great website, it is vital that if you want to reap the rewards—financial and otherwise—of being known as a thought leader, you must produce content that reflects your thought leadership. Doing so on platforms other than your own can start to give you gravitas. Here's how:

- **Books.** There is no better calling card than your own book. Now, is writing a book and getting it published difficult? You bet. As mentioned, it took Martha Stewart five years to get her first book published, and she was 41 when *Entertaining* came out. Was it worth the wait? She probably thinks so. You may have a lot of competitors in your world, but it is safe to say that most of them have not been published, and that is because writing and getting a book published is not easy. If it were, everyone would do it. But if you are able to, you will set yourself apart forever, burnish yourself as an expert's expert, and that's when things will really start to get interesting.

Self-Publishing

Another one of the great things about the digital revolution is that if you want to write a book, you don't need a traditional publisher anymore. Self-publishing allows you to write and print books on your own. Now, of course there are many things a publisher offers that self-publishing does not, including much more credibility, marketing expertise, distribution, and a lot more, but as a way to get started in the brand-building business, self-publishing can work.

- **Podcasts.** Having your own podcast in which you share your opinion and interview other industry leaders is insta-credibility. Similarly, becoming a guest on other podcasts gives you an even greater patina of authority and influence.
- **Speaking.** Speeches and webinars are very powerful ways to show and share your expertise. That they can be recorded and posted on your site or social media makes them all the more useful.
- **Videos.** The same idea applies again here.

Appear in the Media

"The media" has changed so much in the past decade that it is difficult to pigeonhole it. That said, these days it includes, but is not limited to:

- Television
- Terrestrial radio
- Satellite radio
- Magazines
- Newspapers
- Books
- Movies
- Recordings
- Websites
- Blogs
- Social media
- Podcasts
- Speeches and webinars

Yep, there are many, many places where you can start to share your expertise and burgeoning brand. And, as indicated, they are all looking for quality content. If you can offer that, you will get booked and start to grow your profile.

Insider Tip

Google Alerts (https://www.google.com/alerts) let you see what is being said and written about you online. "Twitter search" (https://twitter.com/explore) does much the same for its site. By following these prompts, you can positively inject yourself into any online conversation about you, your services, your industry, and your business.

This then begs the question, how in fact do you get booked or hired?

All shows and websites have bookers, producers, or editors. A quick search on Google or LinkedIn will help you find the right people for the show you want to get on. Websites have About pages that will tell you whom to contact. Once you locate the correct contact, your job is to pitch yourself.

Your other option is to hire a public relations firm. The advantage of this is that PR firms have contacts and relationships with exactly the right people. They can save you a lot of time and effort and quickly help you get booked. Are they expensive? Yes, but then again, so are you (or you will be so soon). Hiring experts puts you a step ahead.

Have a Significant Social Media Presence

If this is not a sign of the times, I don't know what is: although I write a column for *USA TODAY*, when potential corporate sponsors contact me for potential engagements, they are often more interested in my social media following than my column reader-ship numbers.

Social media is fundamental to the would-be influencer for three reasons: First, as Ramon Ray indicated, it is an incredible tool for creating a community of like-minded people who share your passions. Second, social media is a powerful way to get your thought leadership content out there. You can post arti-cles, videos, webinars, speeches, podcasts, infographics—really, any sort of content that you create. And once you post it, and if it's up to snuff, your tribe will share it. *That is how you start to get known.* Finally, once you begin to get a significant following, people and companies will start to seek you out, offering oppor-tunities that you could only have dreamed of when you started this process.

Be Unique and Memorable

There is no shortage of competition in the world today for people's eyeballs. It seems as if everyone wants your attention. One way then for you to stand out from all of the other influencers, thought leaders, and brands vying for that attention is to give people some-thing unique to remember you by.

It could be a physical characteristic, a style of dress, or even a tagline. Consider:

- Steve Jobs wore nothing but jeans and long-sleeve black T-shirts. He maintained having that as a uniform saved time, but it didn't hurt that it also became a dress code for "cool, rich, tech geek."
- Ironically, Sia's hair over her face makes her instantly recognizable.

A personal tagline is also definitely a great way for those of us who are not uber-famous to get people to remember the brand we seek to create. On his blog, Seth Godin gives these examples:

- "I change the people who stop at my desk, from visitors to guests."
- "I give my boss confidence."
- "I close sales."

After writing *The Small Business Bible*, I began to use the tagline, "The country's leading small business expert." Then the coolest thing happened: I began to get introduced that way.

Personal branding works.

So this is the secret: You start by homing in on your unique expertise and perspective and creating thought leadership content that you then parlay into media appearances and more gigs.

As a result, more people will start to learn about you and your brand, and the more that happens, the more big brands are going to want to work with you. Soon, they will then begin to offer you bigger paydays because they will want to be associated with your well-known brand, knowing that it will be able to help them spread their message to their desired market.

So, yes, creating a better-known personal brand can become a very lucrative profit center for you. But do you want to know what is even better than having a lucrative profit center?

Having multiple lucrative profit centers.

How do you do that? By reading Chapter 6, that's how.

BOOM YOUR BUSINESS BOTTOM LINE

▶ If you really want to get big money clients, the best way is by becoming an identifiable, unique brand that people will seek out. You have to become brandtastic.

▶ A great brand, be it personal or corporate, is very specific. It attracts some people, but not others. That's fine, good even.

▶ If you want to become known as a thought leader, you have to first do two things: (1) You need to create thought leadership content—videos, blogs, books, and the like. (2) You have to share it, and your expertise, via the media. Whether that entails hiring a PR agent or doing it yourself, the key is to get out there and get known.

▶ The last step is to create a large social media following because, frankly, that's what people look at these days.

CHAPTER 6

CREATE MULTIPLE PROFIT CENTERS

We cannot direct the wind, but we can adjust the sails.

—Dolly Parton

Let's consider an alternate universe.

Imagine a world where Steve Jobs had a smaller vision and Apple still only made quirky personal computers. No iPhone. No iTunes. No iPad. In this weird world, Ray Kroc never stumbled upon McDonald's, so that little hamburger stand never did invent the Big Mac, the Filet-O-Fish, or the McRib. In this strange place, Richard Branson never thought any bigger than owning a record store, and that was the only business he and Virgin ever created.

Would they even be Apple and McDonald's and Virgin?

No, of course not.

If those giant companies had stuck with the one thing that got them started, we probably would never have heard of them. They might not even be around today. And if they were still around, what would they be? Apple would probably be nothing more than a niche player in the tech world. McDonald's would consist of a couple of burger joints in Southern California. And Virgin would probably be nothing but a tiny retro record shop in London.

So why are you still selling the same one or two products or services that you have always sold?

What Apple, McDonald's, Virgin, and countless other great businesses—large and small alike—have learned is that one of the secrets to booming a business is that you have to create new revenue streams (multiple profit centers).

THE CONCEPT

That you are reading this book means one thing we know is you have already figured out the first critical step to sustaining a business: you created a recipe for success.

An entrepreneur starts a business because he or she has a vision. Either it is a vision to be their own boss, or to start a certain type of business, or something altogether different than that. But whatever it is, the vision strikes, and the business must be born, and so it is.

That's the fun part.

However, once the startup stage is over—the plotting and planning and talking and doing—then things get real. Then you have to figure out how to pay the bills and make a consistent profit. You did that, too. You created some solid strategies that work for your business. It might be a product that sells well, or a social media campaign, or a sidewalk sale, but whatever it is, you figured out something that works for you.

Your Recipe

Let's call this your "small business success recipe"—the strategy or strategies that you use time and again to create a desired result. Like a baker, your recipe is how you make your dough (groan, I know!). A business recipe is a beautiful thing because it can be relied upon again and again for consistent results. It is foundational.

Unfortunately, the issue too many small business people have is that they create a recipe, use it, master it, and then beat it into the ground and never take the time or make the effort to learn another one. Because these one-trick ponies do not have more up their sleeve, they either never grow or they shrink because things peter out or tastes change.

Having only one or two money making recipes is dangerous. First, there *is* a business cycle; things are always fluctuating. Recessions happen. Also, customer habits *do* change. Something that works today may not tomorrow. Krispy Kreme was hot until it was not. Also, there are changes that are beyond your control. The recipe that worked so well the past few years might utterly fail in, say, a pandemic.

As such, the first reason why having multiple profit centers makes so much sense is that it reduces your risk. Having multiple streams of income means that even if one part of your business is down, another part could be up.

Take Nike, for example. The Oregon athletic wear company is of course famous for inventing the running shoe. But Nike is so much more than just a running shoe company now. Its vast empire includes everything from athletic footwear to apparel to all manner of sports equipment and endorsements.

The point of all of this is diversification. For instance, football is a fall sport, so sales of that equipment are up then. When football swag dips in the winter, basketball sales take its place, and then baseball in the spring. Multiple profit centers means sales year-round.

In 1971, Nike cofounders Phil Knight and Bill Bowerman had just launched their company and were trying to figure out how to make a unique running shoe (Bowerman was the track and field coach at the University of Oregon).

Bowerman was having breakfast with his wife one morning, and she was making waffles. He looked at the waffles, and then at the waffle iron, and that is when inspiration struck. Bowerman ran into the basement, got some polyurethane, came back upstairs, and poured it onto the waffle iron.

And that is how the legendary Nike "waffle sole" edition running shoe was born.

Multiple Profit Centers Create Growth

The other reason that it is vital to have multiple profit centers is that this is how you grow. For example, instead of being stuck selling records, you are taking people into space on Virgin Galactic for $250,000 a pop.

That is why, in order to guarantee a steady income stream, you need to be like Nike and Virgin and create several moneymaking strategies—or "multiple profit centers" as Barbara Winter refers to it in her great book *Making a Living Without a Job.*

Having multiple profit centers is like being a good investor. Savvy investors would never own just one stock or one sector. It's too risky. Instead, they diversify their portfolio. The same concept holds true for savvy entrepreneurs. By creating multiple income streams, great entrepreneurs diversify their business portfolio.

A Tasty Example

Oreos. We all love them (right?) Yet, heading into the 100-year anniversary of the iconic product, executives at Oreo knew that doing the same thing they had always done would not cut it for such an important, auspicious occasion. They needed to mix things up.

So, what did they do?

They created a new profit center.

Specifically, for the 2012 centennial anniversary of this sweet sandwich of love, the executives at Oreo decided to do the theretofore unthinkable—they would introduce a new flavor of Oreo.

Meet Birthday Cake Oreo.

Such a smashing success was it that the executives decided this had to become more than a one-time deal, and thus the limited-time flavored Oreo was born. Oreo has since introduced 65 different flavors of its signature cookie, including:

- Root Beer Float Oreos
- Blueberry Pie Oreos

- Peeps Oreos
- Wasabi Oreos (available in China only)

New Oreo flavors equal new buyers equal a new profit center. While that is, of course, good news, according to a report in the *New York Times*, that is not really the main objective of these new products. Instead, the new cookies build the brand, excite customers, and eventually help sell the original.

As Justin Parnell, senior executive of the Oreo brand, says, "When we do it well [introduce a new flavor], it drives our classic Oreo cookie, as well as the sales of the limited edition." The strategy works well. Typically, according to the story, when a new flavor is introduced, sales of the original shoot up 22 percent.

> *Oreo's innovation dream team includes marketers, product developers, researchers and food scientists. The team begins each new Oreo ideation period with a suite of 50 flavor options, and narrows them down to about a dozen. It takes 24 months to introduce a new flavor.*[1]

This makes a lot of sense, doesn't it? Launching a new profit center extends your brand into new markets, and the people who discover those products discover your brand in the process and just may look to see what else you do. It's synergistic.

HOW TO CREATE MORE PROFIT CENTERS

The multiple profit center concept applies equally to the small business as it does to the large corporation, as much to the solopreneur as to the CEO. For example, if you own a computer repair shop, you could begin to seek out corporate clients or offer computer training seminars via Zoom to executives. An added bonus of this strategy is going from B2C (business to consumer) to B2B (business to business), which is in line with our "get bigger clients" model. Or, if you run a family-owned farm, you could add a petting zoo, a gift shop, a farm-to-table restaurant, and a greenhouse. A pizza joint could create a to-go window, a catering division, offer pizza-making lessons, and launch a "make your own pizza at home" product.

There are endless ways to boom your business by adding multiple profit centers to your portfolio, whether you're a computer repairman, a farmer, or a restaurant owner.

It's a four-step process.

Step 1: Consider Your Brand and Business

What does *not* generally work is to come up with a new profit center that is outside of your wheelhouse. Such endeavors take too much time, effort, money, and resources. Oreo created more Oreos, not chicken wings.

What you want are new income sources that align with what you already do. Going that route serves two purposes:

- First, it taps into your personal, or your company's, skill set. Creating a profit center that utilizes your already existing resources saves time and money.
- Of equal, if not more, importance is that a profit center that fits your brand will not confuse your customers or the public. A backyard barbecue store can easily add related items like spas, decking, and so on. It could host barbecue competitions. But the Chinese restaurant that begins to advertise "American Breakfasts!" is missing the point.

Be creative, cast a wide net for ideas, and then begin to vet them. A great additional profit center is one that fits your business and brand, that is not too difficult or expensive to launch, is one that can turn a profit fairly easily and quickly, and is something that extends your reach into new arenas, thereby exposing your business to new customers.

One company that is great at creating new profit centers is Virgin. Here is what Virgin founder and CEO Richard Branson has to say about the concept:

> *When we start a new venture, we base it on hard research and analysis. We put ourselves in the customer's shoes to see what could make it better. We ask fundamental questions: Is this an opportunity for creating a competitive advantage? What are the competitors doing? Is the customer confused or badly served? Is this an opportunity for building the Virgin brand? Can we add value? Is there an appropriate trade-off between risk and reward?*[2]

Step 2: Examine Your Options

Essentially, you have two options when launching additional profit centers: you can launch a new product or service, or you can expand into new markets and locations.

Tom's of Maine did both. The company began by selling natural toothpaste in, of course, Maine. It then added additional products that made sense for the brand, and then expanded nationwide. Today, Tom's of Maine sells products in three general categories: oral care, deodorants, and bath and body. You will notice that it doesn't sell furniture. Not a fit.

Remember, a great brand attracts some people and *repels others*. Tom's of Maine is looking to sell to people who value premium healthy products. It is not interested in selling to people who don't appreciate organic.

The other option is to sell in new markets, either online or off. If you don't have an e-commerce presence, then starting one would be smart. You could begin to sell on Amazon, eBay, or Etsy. Or you could launch your own e-commerce store on your website. Offline, you could open a new location, or start exporting overseas.

Going Global: Make the World Your Business

According to Laurel Delaney, the author of *Exporting: The Definitive Guide to Selling Abroad Profitably,* and founder of GlobeTrade.com, in an increasingly interconnected world, going global is a profit center that many small businesses should consider. Says Laurel,

> *Going global helps any company scale, increase revenue and profitability, stay relevant, and outlive local competitors.*
>
> *Those who go global grow faster, are more productive, and achieve better market performance than their domestic counterparts. But becoming successful at going global takes persistence and a serious commitment. By preparing thoroughly and building business relationships over time, global trailblazers can lay the groundwork for extraordinary sales and success.*
>
> *The current business climate is characterized by speed, change, and chaos. By transforming yourself into a global player, you can learn so much, gain new perspectives, and reap the rewards. No matter where you are at on your journey, taking the first step toward going global will be the thrill of your life, strengthen your business, and pave the path to success. Go forth and make the world your business.*

You can learn more about how to go global at www .globetrade.com and www.womenentrepreneursgrowglobal .org.

Step 3: Start Small and Test

The beauty of booming by beginning a bonus business is that, because it is an extension, it should be neither a big risk nor an expensive one. Indeed, one thing I have learned over the years is that great entrepreneurs are risk-takers, yes, but they are smart, prudent risk-takers. There is no reason to bet the barn on a new profit center and every reason not to.

So, to the extent possible, start small, test, see what works and what does not, and go from there.

Maybe the best additional profit centers to test are those that, once launched, can generate income on their own, without you having to do much more. Money while you sleep is, as we know, a concept that really is quite attractive. You could, for example:

- **Monetize your website.** Add Google ads to your site. People click them and Google pays you money. You could find sponsors who want to advertise on your site. What about e-commerce? People buy, you earn. Or add affiliate links to your site; the affiliates pay you for every lead your site sends their way.
- **Buy rental income.** Rental properties earn money in two ways: the rental income is one way, of course, but almost better is the appreciation the property generates over the years.
- **Join the sharing economy.** Airbnb your spare room. Rent out your car with a service like Turo or Getaround. Lease that empty office space.
- **Generate royalties.** If enough people buy this book, I will be getting royalties for years to come (and thank you very much!). You can do it too. Musicians, writers, artists, podcasters, creators, and inventors all receive royalty income. Or just go on *Shark Tank* and do a deal with Mr. Wonderful!

Step 4: Ready, Aim, Launch!

Once you have brainstormed, considered your brand and business, and tested a few new ideas, you should have a very good idea about what your best bets are. Now is the time to go for it.

Yes, great entrepreneurs are prudent risk-takers, but this time, the operative word is not "prudent" but "risk-taker." Part of what makes entrepreneurship so fun is the risk involved. That new idea may work, but it may not. The only way to know is to commit and jump into the deep end.

That, as they say, is why we play the game.

BOOM YOUR BUSINESS BOTTOM LINE

▶ Every successful business has a success recipe; that is, a consistent way of generating revenue. But the best businesses have several recipes; they create multiple profit centers.

▶ To be successful, additional profit centers must be a logical extension of your business and brand. That way, not only will they not seem confusing to the public, but they will also tap into your company's core competencies and expertise.

▶ Creating new profit centers is essentially a matter of: (1) brainstorming, (2) testing the best ideas, and (3) rolling out those ideas that tested best.

PART II

CRUSHING IT ONLINE

Whether you want to get a million hits on your website or a six-figure social following, the digital ideas and strategies presented here will help you crush it online.

CHAPTER 7

GET ONE MILLION HITS

When I am working on a problem, I never think about beauty,
but when I have finished, if the solution is not beautiful,
I know it is wrong.

—R. Buckminster Fuller

There was a time not so long ago where you could just be an entrepreneur. That is, if you owned a business, it was enough to be visionary and enthusiastic, smart and hardworking, skilled and committed.

No longer.

No, these days that is not enough.

Today, if you want to succeed in business, you need to be two-thirds entrepreneur and one-third geek because, as we all know, business and life today are dominated by the internet. If you don't know what works online and on your website, it is very difficult to succeed, let alone boom your business.

Of course, you very likely know the basics. The essence of a good website is having a clean design, great content or products, digital marketing, search engine optimization (SEO), and similar internet voodoo.

But what takes a site from good to great? How do you go from a few thousand hits and visitors to a million or more? That's the question.

OPTIMIZATION +

Gina Ozhuthual started her business, Bohemian Mama, and website, bohemianmama.com, out of her garage in 2015. In the six years since then, she has completely revamped the site twice, growing and making it bigger and better each time.

Did it work?

You bet. And what Gina did, you can do too.

During the pandemic year of 2020, *she grew her business more than 300 percent*, with almost two million visitor sessions (hits), and that was on top of 200 percent growth the year before. And that 2020 growth is all the more impressive considering the fact that Gina had to completely revamp her inventory that year as her customers' buying habits completely shifted during COVID-19.

Pre-pandemic, the niche for Bohemian Mama was in selling sustainable, ethically sourced products for mother, children, and home. Seventy percent of the product line was geared toward mom, 30 percent toward the kids and home.

But then the bogeyman invaded our lives in 2020 and everything changed.

Almost overnight, as their lives changed, customers of Bohemian Mama completely shifted their buying habits. Consumers were buying less traditional work clothes and more loungewear, and more toys and products for kids who were suddenly at home more.

So Gina flipped the script too. In short order, her online store began to carry 60 percent products for kids and home, 40 percent for mom. And to do so, she had to revamp her site once again. This shift paid off significantly, fostering a loyal customer base paid dividends in more ways than one. Not only was she able to earn a substantial income from the site, Gina also came to learn what her customers wanted from her online store. Each new iteration of the site refined her concept and made it ever more inviting and popular.

"As far as site growth strategy, it is really a recipe of sorts," she explains. "And leveraging all channels effectively is key. This requires working knowledge and dedicated focus on paid media, Google shopping, SEO, social media, email marketing, and now SMS. A website is a living creature and will never be 'set it and forget it.' It requires constant monitoring and attention."

Gina Ozhuthual did many things right on her way to creating a beloved small business website that boomed, even in a pandemic. Great products, listening to her customers, SEO, pivoting, great customer service—it all played a role, but for starters, critically, her site was built on a solid foundation that she was able to scale.

COMMENCING COUNTDOWN, ENGINES ON

If you want to build a site that will take off, for starters, it has to be created on the right platform and designed well. Take it from me—I learned this particular lesson the hard way. My team and I have created and run websites for several Fortune 500 companies, as well as the two we run for my businesses: MrAllBiz.com, my personal branding site, and TheSelfEmployed.com, my "supersite" for all things small business.

On both, the design we began with was a far cry from the design we have ended up with. Why? Because, as Gina Ozhuthual states, a website is a living thing that needs attention and updating, and, beyond that, I made some rookie mistakes on my sites that I don't want you to repeat; they didn't do what I needed them to do, namely get and keep traffic.

On TheSelfEmployed, for example, I was raw and dumb enough when I started that I hired a designer who created a boring design using an increasingly less-used program called Joomla. Two strikes right out of the gate. I hired a new designer, Abby, to fix what the first designer got wrong, and she did. We redesigned the site, and Abby fixed the bugs. Traffic tripled in a year once we got the platform right (WordPress) and the design fixed. Our bounce rate dropped significantly too.

*Bounce rate: The percentage of visitors to a particular
website who navigate away from the site after viewing
only one page. A rising bounce rate is a sure sign
that your homepage is boring or off-putting.*
—Oxford Dictionaries.com

Needless to say, without good design, your site is going nowhere fast. No amount of fancy SEO or digital marketing will make a difference if the site it points to is one that users can't use or don't like.

What is bad design? Generally speaking, it is design that is unattractive and confusing, jarring even. 404 errors abound. The interface is not intuitive. Navigation is a nightmare. Clicking around and getting to where you want to go—or even knowing where you want to go—is difficult. Bad design: you know it when you see it.

Conversely, good design is also fairly self-evident, but definitely contains the following:

- **An attractive user interface.** The design makes sense, flows, and is visually appealing.
- **Easy on the eyes.** The graphics are clean, and the font is large enough and readable. Avoid outdated fonts like Times New Roman or kitschy fonts like Comic Sans.
- **Fast loading.** Slow-loading sites equal sites with a high bounce rate; that is, people leave the site quickly. Maybe worse, Google dings slow-loading sites. Conventional wisdom is that people give a site three seconds to load before moving on.
- **Intuitive navigation.** Like Goldilocks' porridge, you don't want too many navigation tabs nor too few. It needs to be just right.
- **Standard pages.** People have come to expect certain webpages and design elements laid out in certain ways, including a Home page, About, Contact, and Search function.

When I asked my resident tech and design expert Abby what she considered *the most important factors* that lead to quantum e-growth, she said that the key to site growth and scalability isn't just SEO or the site's back-end technology (WordPress, Shopify, etc.). And it is not having a flashy design. While these things certainly do help, Abby says that the user experience (UX) is and should be the number one priority.

The User Experience Should Be the Number One Priority

She says, "If people come to your site and can't find what they're looking for almost immediately, or if it is cluttered and difficult to navigate, they will leave after a few seconds."

As such, she says, the top sites on the web "keep their front-end designs as simple and bare-bones as possible. This is especially true for e-commerce giants like Amazon and eBay. They invest in the best UX designers, because that above all is what has been shown to boost sales and conversions."

Abby's point is well taken. if you want a site that will take off, it needs to be clean, crisp, simple, and useful—all of the front-end basics must be right. It must have the back end right as well. That means the platform the site is built upon has to be one that is easy to work with, fast-loading, and scalable.

When building a site that will scale, you have three options:

1. You can build it yourself, using a platform like WordPress. This option is not recommended unless web design is your thing. If not, using one of the next two options is much better.
2. Go to a website builder site. There are a lot of these out there, such as Yahoo Small Business, Wix, and GoDaddy. They are great because they have built-in templates and point-and-click systems that make building a great-looking site very easy.

3. You can hire a designer to build your site. If you do, while there are a lot of web design options available, it is safe to say that Shopify is great for e-commerce, and for content, WordPress is the best. They are also very affordable.

> 41% of the web is built on WordPress. More bloggers,
> small businesses, and Fortune 500 companies use
> WordPress than all other options combined.
> **—Wordpress.com**

Users of WordPress to create their websites include CBS, Spotify, TED, and the *New York Times*.

BLASTOFF

Broadly speaking, there are two types of traffic that come to a website: organic and paid. With organic traffic, people find your site organically (obviously), via a Google search, by clicking a link on another site, or via a social post. With paid traffic, people find your site by seeing an ad that you have placed somewhere, clicking on it, and then being directed to your site.

Of these two, by far the fastest way to get more people to your site is through paid traffic. Buy an ad, place it, get clicks. That is how it works. As such, buying ads to generate traffic creates targeted traffic far more quickly than any organic option. But paid traffic is, by definition, more expensive. Organic traffic is better because it is free. The downside is that it takes longer to create traffic this way. We need to look at both.

There are seven specific ways that people find a website:

1. **Organic search.** People type a query into a search engine and find your site.
2. **Direct traffic.** Someone types your URL into a browser or clicks a bookmark.

3. **Referral traffic.** Someone clicks a link to your site while viewing content on another site.

4. **Social.** You post a link to your content on a social site and someone clicks on it.

5. **Email.** You send out a weekly e-newsletter and people click on an article or video.

6. **Paid search.** You pay to have your content ranked higher in a search result.

7. **Display ads.** As opposed to a search result, here you advertise on other sites using, say, Google Ads with a display ad. Someone sees your ad, likes it, and clicks on it.

ORGANIC TRAFFIC

Organic traffic is great for all sorts of other reasons aside from cost. For starters, it is targeted; that is, people who type a search query into Google and find the answer on your site are far more likely to like your site, opt in, sign up, subscribe, swipe, click, and buy.

Additionally, ranking high in an organic search result lends added credibility to your site, which means there is a higher likelihood of converting a website visitor into a paying customer when he or she comes from an organic search query.

Here are two great ways to monitor your organic search results:

First, log in to your Google Analytics and look at Acquisition > All Traffic > Channels > Organic Search. This tells you how many of your site visitors come from search engine results.

The other way is to look at the Google Search Console tool (https://search.google.com/search-console). Click over to Performance > Search Results > Queries. This will show you which keywords from your site led people to it and how many visits you received.

In the world of organic traffic, there are a few tricks that stand out and work well. Master these and you can rocket past the Moon on your way to Mars.

Have Great Content

"Content is king" is a maxim almost as old as the internet itself. And that's because it's true. Having great content on your site offers a multitude of benefits:

- **It is great for SEO.** Google loves good content and rewards sites that have it.
- **It generates loyalty.** People return again and again to sites with great content.
- **It fosters sales.** People trust sites with good content, and that in turn can lead to conversions.
- **It's great for social media.** Whether it's blogs, articles, infographics, videos, podcasts, or pictures, social media thrives on the sharing of good content.

Because the creation and distribution of great content is in fact so important today, the next chapter is devoted specifically to that.

Have a Sticky Site

For a site to be popular, it has to be, in the parlance of the internet, "sticky." What is that? It means the site is one people want to visit time and again and is so engaging that when they get there, they want to stick around.

We have all been on sticky sites—and non-sticky ones too. The latter are the worst, aren't they? The one that says "©2016" at the bottom and that, in fact, seems like no one has been there since 2016. The few articles on the site are out of date, and those darn 404 error messages proliferate.

Instead, what we want is a sticky site. That's a site that contains any or all of the following:

Great products and design. You will only stay, shop, and come back to a site if it is easy to find great products you love, and they are displayed cleanly and intuitively. The UX has to be right.

Videos. Videos are just about *the* most engaging kind of content you can have on your site. Fifty-five percent of people watch video online every day, and 95 percent of them retain that information, as compared to 10 percent for text.[1] What kind of videos could you create? So many! Explainer videos, webinars, tutorials, interviews, product reviews, testimonials, demonstrations, or presentations for starters.

Blogs and articles. Mostly, people do one of three things on a website: they read something, they watch something, or they buy something. In terms of reading, you obviously therefore need to give them something good to read, and make sure you update that content regularly if you want to get the SEO benefits.

Podcasts. Yes, it does seem like everyone has a podcast these days, but that shouldn't dissuade you. Podcasts are great because people love listening to them, so they usually will spend quite a bit of time doing so, and that means they will spend more time on your site and then come back to listen to more podcasts. (Sticky, see?)

According to DiscoverPods.com:

32 percent of all Americans have listened to a podcast in the past month.

83 percent of podcast listeners listen for more than seven hours a week.

56 percent of people bought something after hearing it advertised on a podcast.[2]

Aside from having this sort of content on your site, the other way to know if it is sticky or not is via your analytics. Specifically:

- **A low bounce rate.** Because a high bounce rate indicates that people leave your site quickly, the lower the better. How low? Most bounce rates are between 30 percent and 70 percent. If you are below 50 percent, that is remarkably good. But even 70 percent is OK. Above that and you are in trouble.
- **Time spent on site.** The more time people spend on your site the better. The average time spent on a website is 58 seconds.
- **Pages visited.** You want a site where people bop from page to page. On average, a visitor will see two to three pages before surfing on.
- **Quick loading.** The quicker the better. Three seconds or less.

Use Search Engine Optimization (SEO)

I have mentioned SEO several times in this book and in this chapter, and I will mention it several times more because it is that important. While no one expects you to become an SEO expert, having a good working knowledge of how SEO works is important to having a site that goes boom.

The essence of SEO lies in three areas: (1) crawling, (2) indexing, and (3) ranking.

The way it works is this: You create a website and a "search engine spider" from Google (or Bing or some other search engine) discovers your site and automatically analyzes it; this is called "crawling." The search engine then categorizes (or indexes) your site within its system. Then, when someone searches for something, the search engine compares its indexed sites to the search query and serves up the sites that it determines best answer that inquiry. That is the ranking. If you get crawled, indexed, and have content that matches the query well, you will be ranked high.

Keep in mind that SEO is a marathon, not a sprint. It takes a while for your SEO efforts to pay off, but it's worth it. Once an article or page on your site begins to rank high, you will reap traffic rewards for literally years to come.

So, just how do you get Google and other search engines to find your site, like it, and rank it high? Whole books and seminars have been written on the subject, and I would encourage you to seek them out, but that said, there are some basic things you can do to make sure your site begins to rank higher and higher. Let's dive in.

Use Add-Ons

Make sure you use a back-end SEO extension tool. For instance, among the other great things, WordPress offers website owners a plethora of SEO tools that help analyze content and optimize it for search. (Yoast SEO is the one we use.)

Claim Local Listings

For a site and business that is local, an easy SEO win is to claim local listings. Several big, important sites have curated listings for local businesses—Google, Yelp, Facebook, Tripadvisor, and OpenTable in particular, with the two most important being Google and Yelp.

By claiming your local listing, you can add pictures, hours of operation, and other valuable SEO and consumer information. Even better, according to Womply.com, *small businesses that claim their local listings make 58 percent more money.* For SEO purposes, by claiming these listings, you increase your visibility within those categories, and to those sites. And let's just say, there is nothing wrong with Google noticing your business.

Roughly 50 percent of Google's almost 4 billion daily searches are local, and roughly 20 percent of Google searches relate to location.[3]

Use Video

The statistics regarding the popularity of video online verge on the incredible. Here is a small sampling:

- Videos posted on social media "generate 1,200 percent more shares than text and images combined."
- On Facebook, a video receives 135 percent more reach than a photo.
- "Video marketers get 66 percent more qualified leads per year."
- On a landing page, videos increase conversions by at least 80 percent.[4]

But for our purposes right now, here is the stat to know: *A website is 53 times more likely to reach the front page of Google if it includes video.*

Copy What Works

Yes, of course there are all sorts of tips and tricks that people use to "beat" Google, but the fact is, Google constantly changes its algorithm, and keeps it secret, so the chances of outthinking Google are slim. Instead, just keep this in mind: *Google likes quality sites and pages.*

If you post great content on your site (see next chapter), Google will see it. If it's really good, other sites will link to that page. Google *really* likes those "backlinks." So what you want is to simply create great content that people like and link to. How do you know what that is, aside from your educated guess?

Here's a pro tip: Go to Ubersuggest.com, a site run by Neil Patel, who is an amazing internet marketing pro. Patel is a New York Times bestselling author, and Forbes has called him one of the Top 10 online marketers. He was also recognized as a top 100 entrepreneur under the age of 30 by President Obama.

His site, Ubersuggest, allows you to see what pages on what sites get ranked high. Type in your competitor's URL and see what content *and what keywords* they have that rank high and get plenty of backlinks. Then create your own content for those subjects.

Keywords Are Key

You want to use the keywords and key phrases in your content that people search for. Aside from Neil Patel's tool, you can also find what keywords your customers use to find products and content within your niche by using the Google Ads Keyword Planner tool at Ads.Google.com.

PAID TRAFFIC

Your other option, aside from organic, is to buy traffic. There are five ways you can buy traffic online:

1. **Paid search.** This is where you pay to have your little ad inserted into search results on Google, Yahoo, Bing, etc.
2. **Display ads.** These are ads found on other websites.
3. **Social media.** Increasingly important, ads on social media continue to proliferate. You can place ads on YouTube, Twitter, Instagram, LinkedIn, Facebook, you name it.
4. **Sponsored content.** An article on a website may contain a link that goes to another website. That link is paid for.
5. **Influencer placement.** Most industries have related social media influencers, and there is certainly nothing wrong—and a lot right—with working with an influencer to promote your site, product, or content.

To the purist, buying traffic to grow a site might seem like cheating, but no, it's not. It's smart. Does Coca-Cola advertise? You bet. What about McDonald's? Yep. Microsoft? Of course. Any business that has exploded in size has done so with the help of advertising, and that really is all paid traffic is—it is the placement of ads around the web that people click, which then drives them to your site.

What they find there is up to you, but if it's something good, that paid click can become a customer or return visitor rather quickly.

What is even better is that you can *target and buy the sort of "targeted traffic" that is most likely to turn into real, repeatable, sustainable customers and visitors.* Targeted traffic is traffic that you select based on the type of visitor you want. You can target traffic based on:

- Age
- Gender
- Geography
- Profession
- Marital status
- Interests
- Income

Do you see what a shortcut this is to getting to your desired 1 million visitors?

Instead of creating great content, and SEOing the heck out of it, and posting it on social media and then waiting for all of this to pay dividends, you can simply decide to, say, go onto Facebook and place ads targeted at the people most demographically inclined to like your site.

A caveat is important here. As you will see in Chapter 10, "Get 100,000 Followers," it is very possible to waste a lot of money on cheap tricks that internet hucksters promise will get you a huge following. Do not be fooled. There is a difference between real followers and fake followers, between real traffic and worthless traffic. When you see someone online promising to get you hundreds of thousands of clicks for pennies on the dollar, run, don't walk, in the other direction.

On the other hand, buying real traffic from people who see your ad (or blog or video) is a smart, if not inexpensive, way to grow your site.

For example, say you write a post on your website that you share on Facebook. It gets a lot of organic clicks, making it a valuable piece of content. You can then pay Facebook to "boost" that post so that more people who are akin to your regular visitors (called a "lookalike audience") will see it, like it, click on it, and discover your site.

Instant traffic.

If large, highly successful websites buy traffic, you should too. Digiday looked at some major publishers to see how many ads on Facebook were bought by big websites over the course of a random week. Check out what they found:

1. The *New York Times* was running 72 Facebook ads.
2. Buzzfeed had 82 Facebook ads.
3. *Business Insider* was running more than 2,100 Facebook ads.[5]

Let's dive a bit deeper into places where you can buy legitimate traffic via advertising:

Google ads. Google is Google—the head honcho, the top banana, el Numero Uno. Billions of people use it every day to find everything, including what it is you sell or do. Google is the largest advertising spot on the web.

Not to beat a dead horse or anything, but what is great about Google ads (indeed all of these places) is that you can microtarget your audience so that only the people most inclined to like your stuff will see your ad. That means two things: each click is a qualified lead, and you pay less because your ad is seen by fewer eyeballs.

Bing and Yahoo. Bing and Yahoo teamed up, so an ad on one creates an ad on the other. And because they are less popular sites than Google, their ads are cheaper.

Facebook. Facebook is the second largest advertising spot online, owning almost 20 percent of all online advertising. By targeting viewers by age, race, income, and gender, you can place appropriate ads in front of them, be it text, video, images, or slideshows.

Other social media sites. As mentioned, all social media sites accept advertising. LinkedIn is great for B2B. YouTube of course is incredibly popular, and people often watch videos to the end. Almost three-quarters of Instagram users are under 35, and almost half have professional degrees.[6] Lots of options.

Outbrain and Taboola. If you are a content creator, these two sites are great. They place ads for your content at the end of articles and other relevant places on, amongst other places, large sites like MSN, USA TODAY, and Business Insider.

The final question then is: How will you know when you have landed safely on Planet Website Success? You'll know it when you see it!

BOOM YOUR BUSINESS BOTTOM LINE

▶ Getting 1 million hits begins by building a site on the right platform, specifically one that is easy to use (like WordPress) and that can scale.

▶ Next, it is a matter of having the visible front end of a site be attractive, usable, intuitive, and fast. The user experience (UX) is key.

▶ The next step is to have a lot of valuable content and/or products on the site.

▶ There are two ways to get traffic to a site: Organically, or by paying for it.

▶ Organic traffic works but is slow. It is a matter of creating great content and having a sticky site.

▶ Buying traffic works amazingly well. By advertising your content on sites like Facebook, or with Google, you can get clicks and traffic very quickly.

CHAPTER

CREATING CLICKABLE CONTENT

The worst advice? "Don't listen to the critics." I think that you really ought to listen to the critics, because sometimes they're telling you something is broken that you can fix.

—Stephen King

I want to let you in on a little secret.

The most popular thing I have ever written was a total fluke, and that never ceases to perturb me.

Here's the deal: I have written *a lot*, I mean, a heck of a lot. For starters, I have been writing a column a week for *USA TODAY* for well over 20 years. That is more than 1,250 columns, more than a million words. This is my eighteenth book—let's call that another 1.5 million words. And that doesn't even count all of the e-books, articles, white papers, blogs, and other assorted items I have created for clients.

So how is it that a throwaway column I wrote a decade ago for my website turned out to be the thing that has gotten the most clicks? That is the mystery we are going to solve in this chapter, because creating content that gets clicked is what we want.

Today, almost all businesses create some sort of content. Whether it's articles, blogs, infographics, podcasts, e-newsletters, videos, or social media updates, we all have the same goals in mind, namely, to get people to click on it, like it, and share it. As Guy Kawasaki once said, "Retweets are social media gold."

Indeed, one sure way to take your business to the next level is by creating content that gets clicked. Because the more you create content like that, the bigger and more well-known you, your brand, and your business will become. Clickable content will help you build buzz, sell more, grow more, impress more people, get a bigger following, and kick things up a notch.

THE CULPRIT

The article I wrote that went viral, that has been clicked almost 500,000 times, and that continues to get hundreds of clicks a day, even now, 10 years later, is entitled, "The '5 Guys' Fries Trick That Will Blow Your Mind (and Sales!)"[1]

If you are surprised that that is my most clicked article, well, you are not alone. A marketing column about an East Coast burger chain? And let me just be clear: I am not saying this is the best thing I have ever written, because by far it is not. Nor is it the cleverest, the smartest, the most thoughtful, or remotely the most insightful. But it is interesting, and it does offer a unique take, and it also has a good headline. For starters, those are valuable things in the Wild, Wild West of internet content.

But number one? Still surprising.

Headlines Good, Clickbait Bad

What that article is not, however, is "clickbait." Clickbait is the opposite of the kind of content I am advocating. Good content can make a difference for your business. According to Smallbiztrends .com, clickbait is:

> *a piece of content that intentionally over-promises or misrepresents in order to pull users onto a particular website. Clickbait generally captures users with a*

snappy, sensationalist headline—such as "you won't believe this", or "you'll never guess what happened next"—but then fails to deliver on the user's implicit expectations.

There is a fine line between writing a fantastic headline and writing a clickbait one. The former delivers on its promise and enhances your brand; the latter misleads the reader and diminishes it. So, for starters, when creating content, you want to write a headline that does several things well but does not cross the proverbial line. A great headline should be one that is any or all of the following:

- Intriguing
- Valuable
- Unexpected/unique
- Searchable and findable
- Attention-grabbing
- Makes a promise that you can keep

It should follow that a headline designed just to get clicks cannot fit the above description, because there is nothing authentic about it. If you want to win the day, and especially if you want to woo the largest demographic out there (the millennials), then integrity and authenticity had better be your calling card, because that is what they expect and reward.

Inc.com is one of the best sources of information for the entrepreneur. It is a site that gets millions of monthly hits, and its headlines are almost always engaging. According to the Inc. digital editors, their best-performing headlines have common themes:

- **Immediacy.** Words like *Today, Daily, Now*. Example: "6 Daily Habits of Sales Superstars"
- **Real value.** Example: "4 Scientifically Proven Ways to Be More Productive"
- **Celebrity sells.** Example: "Mark Cuban Swears by This Simple Investment Strategy"

- **Odd numbers.** Example: "4.5 Reasons Why E-newsletters Are a Waste of Your Time"
- **Unique takes.** Example: "Why I Ignored Conventional Wisdom Before Quitting My Day Job"

Now consider the headline of my article: "The '5 Guys' Fries Trick That Will Blow Your Mind (and Sales!)." It checks almost all of these boxes. It is intriguing, different sounding, attention-grabbing, and promises to deliver a benefit, something the potential reader wants—more sales.

It also mentions a famous brand, and that is not insignificant. Mentioning something or someone famous is a twofer:

1. It casts a wider net because more people will know who it is you are referring to.
2. It also has the chance to be linked a lot and ranked higher by search engines.

There is one other headline-writing trick you should know: emotions work. Whatever the emotion—love, lust, fear, joy, anger, kindness—if you can legitimately include it in your headline, the potential for it to hit big is increased. Why? Because we are emotional creatures, and studies show that the content that is shared the most almost always is content that pushes someone's button, for good or ill.

After all, who doesn't love a good kitten video?

BuzzSumo.com analyzed an incredible 100 million headlines on Twitter and Facebook over the course of a few weeks in order to answer the question, "What makes an engaging headline?" They were looking to find what content was shared the most, and their findings are surprising and fascinating.

The most powerful three-word phrase in the headlines was "Will Make You," garnering more than two times the number of engagements (likes, shares, comments) than the next most popular phrase, "This Is Why." Typical headlines include:

- 24 Pictures That Will Make You Feel Better About the World
- What This Airline Did for Its Passengers Will Make You Tear Up—So Heartwarming!
- "Who Wore It Better?" Pics That Will Make You Laugh Out Loud

The next finding was less surprising, but no less important. Emotional headlines also drove engagement. Headlines here (often with relevant pictures) included "Tears of Joy," "Make You Cry," "Give You GooseBumps," and "Is Too Cute."

According to BuzzSumo, the key to headline writing in this regard is that, "The most popular phrase 'will make you' is a phrase that clearly sits *in the center of a headline* as it connects two elements. *Thus it creates the structure by linking something to an emotional reaction.*" (emphasis added)

WHAT IS "GOOD," WHAT IS "BAD"?

Your headline is of course only the start. The real key is to create quality content, content that is good, begging the question: What constitutes good?

For our purposes, good content does two things:

1. It engages the reader, viewer, listener, and it
2. Reflects positively on your brand

Indeed, the content you create and share is a reflection of your site, business, and brand. As such, it'd better be up to snuff. This is not to say that it needs to be perfect, far from it, but if you want your content to move the needle, it'd better be good.

Let me suggest that while "good" is subjective, "bad" is objective. That is, bad content is fairly patently obvious. It is the video that is amateurish (and not on purpose), the blog with misspellings and typos, the social media post that rambles.

A bad article is stuffed with the same words again and again, a piece of clickbait disguising as a blog. Bad content is a waste of everyone's time.

Conversely, while "good" content is more subjective—what is good to you may not be good to me—it is also objective in that good content invariably is engaging, smart (on some level), fun, interesting, unexpected and/or valuable, and well done.

What you should strive to create is good content that is an extension of your brand. Give it your voice and personality. Make it polished and worth someone's time. Think about your audience as you create it, and ask yourself, "What would my people like to know from this?" Your content could be goofy or funny, smart or sophisticated, or cute and kind, but whatever it is, it needs to be in your brand voice.

And if you want it to be clickable and sharable, for starters, it has to be actually, objectively good.

IS CONTENT KING?

An early proponent, and beneficiary, of the "content is king" philosophy was Yahoo. An internet pioneer, Yahoo was founded as a nascent search engine by two Stanford grad students in 1994, and naturally, Jerry Yang and David Filo named it "Jerry and David's Guide to the World Wide Web." A directory of other websites, the guide was renamed Yahoo! in 1995.

Yahoo grew exponentially throughout the late nineties, but *not* due to its guide or any search function, but rather, because it smartly adopted an aggressive agenda of acquiring other companies with superior content and tools. For example:

- In 1997, it acquired Four11, whose RocketMail would become Yahoo! Mail.
- Shortly thereafter, it bought ClassicGames.com, which soon morphed into Yahoo Games.
- The late nineties purchase of eGroups became Yahoo Groups.

- The 1999 purchase of the then-ubiquitous GeoCities eventually became a web hosting service that continues to be one of Yahoo's biggest moneymakers.

Does betting on great content work? You tell me. In the last month of 1999, the value of Yahoo's stock doubled, and in 2008, Microsoft offered to buy Yahoo! for $45 billion.

Yahoo! Fun Facts

- Founders Yang and Filo added the famous exclamation mark at the end of Yahoo because the word *Yahoo* was already trademarked as a BBQ sauce.
- In 2005, for its tenth anniversary, Yahoo gave away coupons to *all Yahoo users* for a free ice cream cone from Baskin-Robbins.
- That same year, 2005, Yahoo invested $1 billion in a hot Chinese startup. Yahoo currently owns 15 percent of this retailing giant that is now valued at more than $30 billion. A little site called Alibaba.

Your X-Factor

Anita Campbell is the founder and CEO of Small Business Trends and the site Smallbiztrends.com. What began as an e-newsletter sent to a few people 17 years ago has blossomed into a content juggernaut with 2.5 million monthly visitors. Anita says that the secret to succeeding with a content strategy is understanding that you need to play "the long game." If you do that—if you create and post content consistently—the payoffs are "geometric."

"It works this way," she told me, "one article can get you, say, a 1x return. And let's say that five articles can net you a 5x return. Then it gets interesting. 10 articles will give you a 20x return,

20 might be a 50x return, and it just grows exponentially like that." She explained that the "x" is multifold. It consists of:

- **SEO.** The more you post, the more search engines will like your content, and the more people who will see your content and learn of your business.
- **Branding.** More people will come to your site from search results, and, therefore, the bigger and better your site and brand will become. People will learn of you and your site and begin to seek you out for additional opportunities.
- **Business.** As a result of the above, your business will grow in ways you cannot predict. As more people learn of you via your content, advertisers want to advertise on your site, corporations will want to be associated with your brand, and people will want to work with you

So, yes, the "x" value that comes from consistently writing and posting good content is consistently multifold.

Anita says that anyone in any field can adopt and reap the rewards of this strategy. These are the steps:

1. **Understand what it is your customers need or want to know.** Whatever it is, you need to begin to create content around that. Anita is partial to written content because "it gets into Google's algorithm easily, and there are no technical requirements, as there are with video shoots, podcasting, and so on." That said, consistently posting great content can certainly be adopted for video, e-commerce, and podcasting too.

Pro Tip: Don't know what people in your world are searching for? Anita Campbell suggests that you begin typing something related to your field into your browser and seeing how Google's Autocomplete looks to complete that query, because "that is what people are searching for."

2. **Establish your thought leadership.** You know things about your field that others don't. Write about that. Learn about what they want to know, and write about that, too. "What is great about this," Anita says, "is that you do not need anyone's permission to begin to become the expert in your field." By writing and publishing content, you will start to be seen as an expert—by your customers, by people in your industry, and by Google.

3. **Share it.** Share your content on your social channels, in e-newsletters, to customers, and on other websites. This too helps establish your gravitas. "Write and share, write and share," she says, "and you will become better known in your field, and additionally, your SEO will reflect this." When Anita speaks about the 10x value of each piece of content, this is what she means.

One last thing: Anita strongly suggested that you not share your content only once. "Social feeds expire quickly. If people don't see your content the one time you post it, they won't see it." Instead she says, post the same content several times, and on different channels.

The key to all of this is great content, consistency, and patience. This is another clue as to why my "5 Guys" article has been so successful. As it has been around now for several years and because it was well written with an intriguing, actionable headline, it got clicked a lot. And because it was clicked a lot, Google ranked it high. And because Google ranked it high, it gets clicked a lot. That 1x value Anita mentions is actually a 500,000x value for me, as that is how many people have found and read it.

This geometrically expanding circle of success is why Anita Campbell's motto is, *"From a tiny acorn, a mighty oak grows."*

CONTENT ALONE IS WORTHLESS

So, yes, as a general rule, "content is king" is true, makes sense, and works. But, that said, it is also a vastly oversimplified maxim.

Content alone, in a vacuum, can help move you forward, sure, but it won't create the sort of quantum propulsion that creates a sonic business boom. No, to do that, your great content has to be paired with a great strategy.

Check it out: If you have great content, but no one can find it, it's worthless. That is like being alone in a dark room; you know you are there, but no one else does. Or, if you wrote something great but gave it a crappy headline, it will never get clicked, read, or shared. Strike two. And if you have great content but it doesn't further your business goals, that's strike three.

So, instead of striking out, it is incumbent upon you to combine your great content with a smart strategy. If you do that, the equation will look like this:

Valuable content + Savvy strategy = Small business home run.

HITTING IT OUT OF THE PARK

OK, so you get the program. To gain traction with your content, to really see the multiple x value of content creation, you need to combine your valuable content with a growth strategy. Any or all of the following strategies are important if you want your content to be found, clicked on, and shared.

1. Mix It Up

Yes, my friend and colleague Anita suggests that you concentrate on written content, and for good reasons. I certainly agree, but I will add in a caveat. Written content is great and, yes, is easy to create. When you look around the web, it is still the main medium of choice. But even within written content, there are many different ways to present your expertise and ideas. There are blogs, articles, e-books, white papers, infographics, case studies, and guides.

Do you know what *blog* stands for? It actually is short for "web log."

But beyond that, people consume information in a variety of ways. Their learning styles are different, and how they like to be entertained varies. Some people primarily process information by listening—they are auditory. Others are visual. Still others seek out written information. Given that, it follows you need to create content using as many modes as possible. Videos, pictures, GIFs, infographics, podcasts—they all should be part of your content mix.

2. People Must Be Able to Find It

For your content to be great, people have to be able to find it, and in this context, "findable" has two meanings:

It Has to Be Findable Within Your Site

This requires internal linking as well as having sidebars such as "You may also like," "What's hot this week," "Popular," and so on. Another easy win is to have a search function on your site so people can find what they are looking for. Finally, be sure to promote your latest and greatest content on your home page.

It Also Has to Be Findable Outside of Your Site

This comes from our old pal, SEO. Essentially, you want the keywords or phrases that people use to search for something to match keywords or phrases in your content or content description. Here are a few more easy SEO to-dos:

- **Your content must be unique.** Google abhors repurposed or already-posted-elsewhere content.
- **Your keyword should be part of your headline.**
- **Make it visual.** Blogs with pictures get 94 percent more views than those without.

- **Link internally.** This is how you get visitors to spend more time on your site.
- **Get incoming links.** Quality links to a site or page is how Google originally determined how high to rank a page. A lot of links from quality sites strongly suggested that page must be valuable. While less important now, it is nevertheless still important and a great strategy. Write for other blogs and link to your site, or reach out to webmasters and suggest a link exchange. Yes, this old saw is still sharp.

What you *do not* want to do is try to outthink Google. For example, there was a time when sites used to "stuff" keywords into pages, hoping to fool Google's search bots into thinking this is actually a good site, given all of the great keywords. Not anymore.

Here's a great SEO tip from Neil Patel: One reason Wikipedia gets consistently ranked so high is that it has so many articles that mention famous people, places, and things, especially company names. Company names are often searched, and so, if you can create content that can organically and logically integrate famous company names and examples, you will gain tremendous SEO value, and clicks.

3. Your Content Must Be Readable, Watchable, Listenable

Neil Pasricha is a very successful Canadian author. A million-seller author. One of his mantras is "Breathable equals readable."

What he means by this is an unreadable piece is one that is so dense, so loaded with words, that people won't read it. The paragraphs that go on for two pages and are 37 sentences long. Pages with no white space. Articles that have no bullet points. Especially today in this e-reading era, content has to be easy on the eyes. The font size needs to be at least 12 points, and the type must be clean and crisp.

Needless to say, variations on this rule equally apply to your video, pictorial, and podcast content. Videos must be well lit, not too long (typically no more than five minutes, and shorter is better); podcasts need to be clear; infographics should not scroll on for two pages.

4. You Need a Sharing Strategy

Facebook changed the game in so many ways, but probably the most significant is the advent of the sharing of content. Suddenly, that lonely—if fascinating—article sitting on that obscure website was not so lonely anymore. With a single click, people were able to share their content to the news feeds of their followers, allowing articles and blog posts to reach an even wider audience.

Social media is truly a game changer, and as such, we have to make it easy for people to share our great content if we want that multiple x factor that happens for Smallbiztrends. This means having Facebook, Twitter, and LinkedIn sharing buttons (at a minimum) next to all of your content.

But sharing is not solely the responsibility of the viewer and reader. It is on you to create a sharing strategy of your own. Elsewhere in this book we will go over this in detail, but right now the important thing is to realize that all of your writing and blogging and filming and editing is for naught if you are not also sharing. A consistent social media sharing strategy is required if you want to hit it out of the park.

5. There Should Be a Call to Action

If you created something truly valuable and memorable, then a lot of people are going to see, read, watch, or listen to it. It would be a big whiff if you lost that opportunity by not giving them more. Either you should give your audience the ability to easily find and contact you, or your content should lead back to your site or social, or it should give them additional products to buy, or another benefit.

But whatever it is, ask for the sale, as it were.

6. You Need to Track Your Content

To find out if all of this content is doing its job, to see if it really is getting you 10x value, you need to track it. Analytics are your friend. Things you need to be sure to track include:

- **Traffic to the page.** This is the basic metric.
- **Engagement.** Social shares, comments, time on page, bounce rate.
- **Conversions.** If you want the content to generate leads or sales or move people into sales funnels (see next chapter), then you need to track where they go after they leave this particular piece of content. If it is driving them to your desired web destination, bingo.

Knowing what content works, and which pieces do not, allows you to double down on the winners. Figure out why certain pieces were popular, and move more in that direction. I stumbled upon this content formula after I wrote that "5 Guys" piece, but we have since used it time and time again to create similarly successful articles (albeit admittedly, not in the stratosphere of that original piece).

An old Japanese proverb goes, "The best time to plant a tree is 20 years ago. The second best time is today." The same goes for your content. It matters little if you are only getting started with this strategy. Why? Because "From a tiny acorn, a mighty oak grows."

BOOM YOUR BUSINESS BOTTOM LINE

► One of the best ways to boom your business is by creating clickable content; content that is interesting, valuable, and/or different.

► Content comes in many forms, and if you want to reach a wide audience you need to create a lot of different types of content—articles, blogs, videos, podcasts, etc.

► One key way to get clicks is to understand how to write headlines that are on the right side of the line between intriguing and clickbait.

► Content alone is worthless, even great content. That content must be both shared (by you) and findable (by others) if you want to boom.

CHAPTER 9

THE DIGITAL DIVIDE

People don't buy what you do, they buy why you do it.
—Simon Sinek

Don Draper had a problem.

It is the last scene of the very first episode of *Mad Men*. We have yet to discover the brilliant, manipulative, smooth-talking, shape-shifting, debonair ad man that is Don Draper. But not for long.

In 1960, when this scene takes place, the dangers of smoking were just becoming widely known. Draper is tasked with the unenviable job of selling Lucky Strike cigarettes. His assignment is being made doubly difficult by the latest FTC rules which mandate that cigarette advertisers can no longer make any health claims such as "low-nicotine" or "filtered tips."

The pitch meeting with the execs from Lucky Strike is not going well. Everyone is lamenting the new rules. Don's boss, Roger Sterling, is (almost) blunt: "You have to realize that through manipulation of the mass media, the public is under the impression that your cigarettes are linked to . . . certain fatal diseases."

The Lucky Strike boss shoots back: "Manipulation of the media? Hell, that's what I pay you for!"

Junior ad man Pete Campbell then pipes up and declares that the campaign should essentially be, "Yes, cigarettes are going to kill you, so just be a man and do what you love." The duly unimpressed

Lucky Strike team gets up and begins to walk out when inspiration strikes Don.

"How do you make your cigarettes?" he asks. Answer: "We breed insect-repellent tobacco seeds, plant 'em in the North Carolina sunshine. Grow it. Cut it. Cure it. Toast it—"

Bingo!

Don writes on the chalkboard: "Lucky Strikes—It's toasted."

It's not a health claim, so it's legal, and yet it gives Lucky Strikes the patina of being healthy, natural. The advertisers' eyes light up, they sit down and the boss says, "It's toasted . . . I get it." (And by the way, "It's toasted" really was the Lucky Strike motto.)

Of course, media manipulation still occurs today, but we are a far cry from the days of Don Draper, when an ad man in a gray suit could create a media campaign that manipulated consumers into buying products that potentially could kill them.

Indeed, between the millennial generation's love of authenticity, the new ethos of transparency, and social media's interactivity, the job of the entrepreneur and marketer is vastly different than it was in Draper's day. Today, your job is not to manipulate and coerce, it is to be authentic and engage.

Beyond that, and maybe just as important, in a world where everyone is online, where we are zooming and texting and emailing and posting, it is harder than ever to make a personal connection. The good news is that there are an array of digital tools available now that allow you to do just that—if you take advantage of them.

But that's the challenge, isn't it? Small business people understandably tend not to be early adopters of technology. We are so busy running our businesses that taking the time and making the effort to learn some new trick often does not seem worth it. And yet, in this case, it is, especially if it can help forge a personal connection in an impersonal digital world.

So, which side of the digital divide are you on?

If you want to build your brand, boom your business, make more money, connect with more people, be relevant, expand your empire, share your content, impress your customers, attract new customers, be authentic, build influence, and make a difference, you should take advantage of these tools. They all work, are fairly easy to adopt and use, and are cost effective.

Specifically, what I am talking about are six different, powerful digital tools that you cannot only use to help forge a more personal connection with your tribe, but that can, at the same time, help you connect to a vast new audience. They are:

1. An opt-in list
2. Funnels
3. Livestreaming videos
4. Videos
5. Podcasts
6. Webinars

And away we go!

CREATE A HUGE OPT-IN LIST

It may seem old-school already in the digital age, but creating an opt-in list is one the best, easiest, and most affordable ways for not only connecting with people, but also sharing your great content and igniting a significant small business explosion. But here's the thing: I am not talking about creating a list of a few hundred people. Instead, what we want is a list of tens or hundreds of thousands. Do that, and you are practically assured of blasting off.

Getting someone to opt in, that is, to give you their email address, creates a rare relationship in the world of marketing. Take an e-newsletter for example. When they opt in to your newsletter, people are *giving you permission to contact them again*. In fact, they *want* you to contact them again; that is the whole point of signing up for a newsletter.

Think about that. How often do people—especially folks who may not be paying customers—ask you to contact them again? Right, not often. But when they opt in, they do.

Consider then what it means to have a list of 10,000 people. Or 100,000. That is 100,000 people who like and want to hear from you or your business. Now say that you are having a sale on your e-commerce site. While yes, you can and should advertise and market that to your regular customers, what if you could also tell a list of 100,000 people—people who are used to getting emails from you—about your sale?

Right, boom!

Needless to say, creating goodwill with your list is the secret to making this plan work (well, actually, creating that massive list in the first place is the other secret, but we will get to that shortly.)

There are a lot of ways to get people to opt in, and some are better than others for creating goodwill.

E-newsletters

Your basic "sign up for our free newsletter" is fine but won't do the heavy lifting that we are looking for. *In order to create a massive list that can get you massive results, you have to give massive value.* Newsletters are a good start, but as you well know, some are better than others. Yours has to be among the best if you want to begin to create a huge list and receive the attendant value it can bring.

Your newsletter needs to be compelling and valuable. It has to have content that people look forward to getting, content that somehow improves their lives or businesses. It cannot simply be a weekly advertisement for your business. Whether you use humor, articles, or videos, having one that is top-notch is how you begin to start generating a big list.

The other thing that really works is to make it personal. Corporate, jargony e-newsletters are a dime a dozen and worth about as much. By writing your e-newsletter (or at least the opening) in the first person and giving it that personal touch, by sharing real stories and insights, you stand a far better chance of generating traction and growing your list.

You can increase the open rate of your newsletter by:

- Having a compelling subject line that uses keywords
- Adding video to it
- Diving into your newsletter analytics to discover the day and time your newsletter gets opened most
- Having a recognizable sender name

A personal newsletter that adds a ton of value to the recipient, which gives more and sells less, is the type of newsletter that can be a good foundation for generating that big list we are after.

Other Opt-in Options

While e-newsletters are nice, as mentioned, they are only a start, a piece of the puzzle. You need to combine that with some of these other options:

- Have a contest—opt in to enter
- Sneak peek of content—opt in to see the rest
- E-book—opt in to receive
- Sign in to comment on an article, blog, video, or podcast
- Freebie—opt in to receive
- Offer extra benefits to subscribers—opt in to get extra content, special discounts, etc.

The other, and very effective, option is to use events and your best digital content as a way to incentivize sign-ups. Webinars, podcasts, and videos are especially useful. Once people see that they will get extra value for opting in—a free webinar or cool video or whatever—resistance begins to melt.

Exploding Your Opt-In List

Last year I was on Facebook one night and saw an ad for a free webinar that promised to show me how I could create a six-figure opt-in email list. Despite my skepticism, I clicked on the ad and ended up watching an hourlong webinar from a guy named Mike Dillard. He explained exactly how he had created an opt-in list of 500,000 people.

500,000.

That got my attention.

As if that alone were not remarkable enough, what also got me is that Mike did not hide the ball during his free webinar, as so many of these free deals seem to do. He explained exactly the process he uses to grow his list. I was so impressed that I plunked down a hefty fee to learn more.

After watching Mike's great course, I decided to grow my own list. I had, then, a list of a few thousand, most of whom came from our e-newsletter and from opt-ins from webinars I present.

I knew there had to be a better, faster way.

So I listened to webinars from other marketers and, as is my wont, read a bevy of blogs and books. The results were pretty impressive. In short order, I was able to grow my opt-in list from a few thousand to more than 40,000.

Here's how:

- First, as so many of these folks wisely suggested, I created a freebie, an e-book. Mine was called *Marketing on a Shoestring*. I advertised it on my websites and on Facebook. People who found it and wanted it were directed towards an online sales funnel I had created.
- Once there, they opted-in to get the book for free, and then were given an option for an upsell: They could join my Facebook group, *Steve Strauss' Shoestring Startup*, for only $7 a month (normally $37.) Such a deal!

It worked. Between the free e-book and the cheap yet valuable group, I grew my opt-in list significantly, and quickly.

Dillard says that the toughest trick with e-marketing is to get people to pull out their credit card the first time. By offering something of substance for a dollar (or seven!), you are moving people into your sales pipeline in an easy, nonthreatening way.

This trick is, as Mike Dillard says, "the keys to the kingdom." If you can master this process of getting people to give their information the first time, you can grow a list into the five and six figures, and once you have that, you are practically assured of success whenever you launch your next product, or speech, or sale. Share whatever it is with your huge list of people who already like you, and they will be inclined to buy.

Do this again and again and you will have created a very profitable business.

It all starts with getting people into that sales funnel.

FUNNELS

A sales funnel in the sense I am using it here is likely different from what you may be thinking.

In the offline world, getting someone into a sales funnel is sort of like when you go shopping for a car. First a salesperson warms you up, then maybe you are handed off to someone else, then the "manager" tells you there is no way they could take your offer, and then you make a deal, and then they bug you forever.

Online, you might be thinking that your website is a sort of sales funnel, and it sort of is. But not. The typical small business website serves multiple functions: brand building, information center, product catalogue, and content marketplace. The site might list some products or services for sale, and those product pages might link to other pages. The company's contact information is listed somewhere. These are all well and good things. The primary purpose of most such sites is informational, *not* to turn a new viewer into a customer who buys at that moment, but that is exactly what an online funnel is designed to do.

When I clicked on Mike Dillard's Facebook ad, I was taken to an online sales funnel, not a website (though it looks like one), and that funnel walked me through a process of watching the webinar, creating trust, getting me to want to know more, and then converting me into a paying customer. Step by step. That is what we are talking about here.

The funnel system that he uses is also the one I use. It is called ClickFunnels.

ClickFunnels is not the only funnel game in town. Other similar sites include:

- Leadpages
- Convertri
- Simvoly

The best way to think of a funnel is as a website except that its purpose is to enroll viewers in a step-by-step, page-by-page process that ultimately leads them to take some action: buy, click, swipe, opt in, watch, read, share.

Just like a website builder, a site like ClickFunnels has a point-and-click system that helps you build the funnel you need.

When you start out, you will see a page (called a "squeeze page") that asks whether you want a funnel that collects emails, sells a product, or hosts a webinar (there are many others). The last funnel I built was to get people to join a private Facebook group I was launching. The first page invited users to gain access by entering their name and email address because my initial goal was to grow my list. The next page explained what the group was about, the next made an offer to join, and the next was checkout.

On one typical day, I had 70 unique people see the first page (the "squeeze page"). Thirty-one were intrigued enough to move on to the next page, the sales page. Roughly two-thirds of those folks (19) wanted to join the group and so moved on to the order form. That's roughly a 36 percent conversion rate, from viewers toward buyers, and that's pretty remarkable.

Does your regular website do that? Mine doesn't.

Another great thing about a funnel site is that you can use all sorts of events to engage people and get them to click through your steps, such as:

- Webinars
- Videos
- Membership groups
- E-commerce storefronts
- Daily deals
- Product launches
- Surveys

So this is the first essential idea. You can dramatically increase the number of people you reach on a regular basis by creating a huge opt-in list. That list begins with regular, organic efforts like getting people to receive your great newsletter, enter a contest, or receive your e-book. You then kick things into high gear by systematically working to grow that list by using a site and service like ClickFunnels. The list that you achieve by creating a funnel profit center like this can be one of the best ways to take your business to the next level.

LIVESTREAMING VIDEO (AND OTHER FACEBOOK TOOLS)

Often referred to as "the Queen of Facebook," Mari Smith is considered one of the world's foremost experts on Facebook marketing and a top social media thought leader. *Forbes* magazine describes Mari as "the preeminent Facebook expert. Even Facebook asks for her help." Facebook hired Mari to teach businesses throughout the United States and to help create the company's Blueprint certification programs. IBM named Mari as one of seven women who are shaping digital marketing.

And today we have Mari helping us.

She says that if you want to connect to customers in an impactful way and stand out in a cluttered digital world, you must look into livestreaming with Facebook Live. Mari says that "Facebook is determined to be a dominant leader in next-generation streaming video platforms, essentially competing with Netflix, Amazon Prime Video, Apple TV+, and YouTube. Mark Zuckerberg has said that YouTube is Facebook's biggest competitor when it comes to video."

With this context in mind, Mari adds, "Facebook Live video typically gets more than six times the reach and engagement than other content types. Facebook actually rewards videos—and Pages that post them—with returning viewers and those who search for you." Beyond that, she says, getting on Facebook Live is a "massive opportunity" due to the lack of competition.

Mari points out that Socialbakers, a leading social media marketing platform, revealed in one of its 2020 social media trend reports that *only 0.08% of worldwide brands on Facebook take advantage of live-streaming videos*. The lack of competition for eyeballs on the site equals a huge opening for the small business person who is willing to come on camera and connect with its audience. "You will create more trust and loyalty," she says, "I have. In fact, I have found Facebook Live video to be exponential in creating solid results for my own business."

If going live on Facebook is not your thing, Mari suggests that you either (1) find someone on your team who could be a suitable spokesperson for your business or, (2) create compelling short video content showcasing your business, product, team, or customers and post it. "Using a platform such as Wave.video or InVideo.io will make it really easy to create striking videos for posting across all your social channels."

When I asked Mari what she thought most small businesses did wrong when it comes to Facebook advertising, her immediate answer was "incorrect targeting." Targeting the wrong audience wastes your time and money. The good news is that, "this is an easy mistake to fix with proper granular targeting using Facebook's advertising platform, specifically when you have a very niche product or service."

Mari also mentioned a Facebook tool she loves, discussed elsewhere in this book, called "Lookalike Audiences." She says that lookalike audiences are "a wonderfully effective way to expand your audience with prospects that are similar to your core audience." Mari gave me the example of an email list that you can load into Facebook. Facebook will use that list to create a lookalike audience that matches your users' profile. "Then you expand upon your top customers using the Lookalike tool."

Mari's final suggestion was to check out Facebook's retargeting tools. "Everyone is busy and easily distracted these days. We don't necessarily make buying decisions the first time we see an ad or an organic post with an offer." Estimates are that 97 percent of people who visit a site leave without buying, and then they are gone for good.

Retargeting solves that. Retargeting puts a cookie on a user's browser so that after they leave the Facebook ad, they will still see the ad again later, while reading an article, listening to music, or visiting some online store.

(Mari clearly knows her stuff. If you need help with your Facebook marketing, I strongly advise you to check out her offerings at MariSmith.com.)

VIDEO

As Mari Smith says, when it comes to having content that engages, video is tough to beat. The ease of creation, affordability, and popularity of online video makes it a perfect vehicle for you to be on the right side of the digital divide; videos are an excellent way to both connect with your current community as well as cultivate a bigger one.

People often talk about "engagement." But what does that actually mean? Essentially, engagement means that your audience takes some action with regard to your posting, content, or product.

Engagement means different things on different social sites. On Twitter, it would be a retweet. On Facebook, it could be a like or a share. Engagement can also mean a click, comment, purchase, view, listen, download, reply, forward, or follow.

The stats do not lie. A 2020 Renderforest survey found that 85 percent of people say that videos help them better connect with a brand, and 44 percent said they are more likely to buy a product after watching a video about it. Video is the most preferred type of content on social media pages (81 percent prefer it), and viewers spent up to 88 percent more time on a site with video.

Aside from great conversion rates and popularity, there are five other reasons why you should consider making video a big part of your get-out-the-vote strategy:

1. **Video builds trust.** In this anti–Don Draper era, where fluff has been replaced by a demand for authenticity, few things offer a better chance to demonstrate that than video. First, because we all watch so much video these days, the medium is familiar and comfortable. Also, being able to look into the camera and talk to people directly is powerful, as is demonstrating a product, or cracking a joke, or interviewing customers.

   The visual intimacy of video can break down the e-barrier.

Millennials were born between 1981 and 1996. Gen Z was born between 1997 and 2012. These two generations now make up almost half of the US population. It is no secret that they are changing the game for businesses given that what they expect is authenticity and transparency.

According to *PR World* (December 28, 2020), "About two-thirds (65%) of millennials say they have boycotted a brand that took an opposing stance on an issue, and 62 percent favor products that show off their political and social beliefs."

Similarly, according to a report on Frontify.com, Gen Z "prefers brands that are authentic. They say *they trust brands that use real people* and are more likely to buy from those brands that support social causes. They're also quick to stop buying brands they think are racist, homophobic, or macho."

2. **Video ranks higher.** Yes, as we have seen, getting a Page 1 Google ranking is tough, but it is less tough if you use video. Moovly.com reports that you have a 53 times better chance of landing on the first page of Google if your page contains a video.[1]

3. **Video promotes brand recall.** HubSpot reports that 80 percent of people can recall a video they have watched in the past month.[2]

4. **Video is mobile-optimized.** How many times have you been on your phone today? Exactly. 90 percent of all consumers watch videos on their phones.

5. **Video is sharable.** Says Forbes.com, "Video content wants to go viral. It is estimated that 92% of people who consume mobile videos share them with other people. Simply Measured discovered that video is shared 1,200% more than both links and text combined."[3]

Last, but as they say, "certainly not least," is just how easy it is to make a good video nowadays. In this iPhone/YouTube era, people are accustomed to watching imperfect videos. This is not to say that yours should be amateurish. They should not. But they need not be flawless, either. Yes, there are times when hiring a professional videographer is the way to go, but for the average "get-the-word-out" video, doing it yourself with some good editing software is the way to go.

So, what exactly can you post videos of? You can post videos explaining a product or service (a.k.a "explainer videos"), product demonstrations, presentations, or recorded webinars. You can also post product reviews, animations, or customer or employee interviews. Whiteboard animation videos are also very popular and, even better, are inexpensive and easy to make on a site like Doodly.com. You have certainly seen these sorts of videos online. They are popular because they are simple, easy to follow, and engaging.

PODCASTS

To say podcasts are popular would be a vast understatement. Check out what Edison Research discovered:

- Every week, more than 50 million people listen to podcasts.
- Those listeners typically tune in to five shows a week, and
- They subscribe to six different podcasts.

In fact, podcasts are so popular that it might seem that almost everyone has a podcast these days, but that should not discourage you. If what we are looking for on this side of the digital divide is to use digital tools to better connect while also letting new people discover us, then having a podcast is tough to beat.

For starters, they can help build your brand. One of the great things about having a podcast is that it helps establish you as an expert in your field, a thought leader. If you are the one with the show, the one interviewing guests, there must be a reason for that, right? They are also a great networking tool. Through interviewing others on your show you cannot only connect with your audience but also meet industry experts and leaders. When your listeners tune in and listen to what you have to say, it's a great way to forge a relationship with your audience.

Podcasts can be lucrative. If you create a show that pops, the income potential from ads and sponsors can be huge (as you will see in a moment).

Podcasts are easy and affordable. You can either launch a podcast yourself using off-the-rack tools, apps, and equipment, or you can have an engineer/producer create the show for you. Either way, it is neither complicated nor costly. A Craigslist search for "audio engineer" or "podcast studio" will land you some good leads for people who can help you or produce your show.

Steps

If you want to create a show yourself, here are the basic steps:

- First, decide on a topic, name, and style for the show.
- Next, you will need some way to record it, either on your own or in a studio.
- The show needs a place to live online, so you will need a host platform. This is similar to a website host. Your best options are Libsyn, Podbean, and SoundCloud.
- You will also need to be able to have the show uploaded to iTunes, SoundCloud, iHeartRadio, Google Podcasts, and all other places where people download podcasts.
- Finally, you will need to market it.

If you want to record a podcast on your own, check out:

- Anchor.fm: Here you can create a show with your iPhone and have it hosted and distributed to all major podcasting platforms.

- Garage Band (on a Mac)
- Adobe Audition
- Audacity

Meet the Master

When we talk about someone using the tools available in this chapter (and book) to build a business and brand, to connect and convince, and a person making a lot of money in the process, we are talking about John Lee Dumas.

In 2012, John started his podcast *Entrepreneurs on Fire* with zero listeners. Now it has more than a million regular listeners each month, and the podcast has made him $14,575,435 in net income. (How do I know this? Every month, John posts his income reports from the show publicly on his website, www.eofire.com/income).

But like all entrepreneurs, John worked hard to get where he is today. After 9/11, John enlisted in the military and served combat duty in Iraq. Afterward, like so many young people, he searched to find his place in the world: doing the corporate cubicle thing, working for a startup in New York, selling commercial real estate in San Diego, and attending a semester of law school. Nothing fit.

It was while listening to a podcast one day (in the nascent days of podcasting) that inspiration struck. John loved entrepreneurship, loved podcasts, and loved the idea of creating something of value to others. Eureka! Launch a show *about* entrepreneurs *for* entrepreneurs.

And so, *Entrepreneurs on Fire* was born.

A show like that, he decided, was how he could best blend his passions and talents. John believes that it is when you combine your interests with your expertise by using the right platform that you are best able to reach your sweet spot, or what he calls, "your zone of fire."

For John, that platform was podcasting. For others, it could be books, blogging, videos, graphics, speaking, or what have you.

Whatever vehicle you choose, JLD (as he is sometimes known), suggests that you look for your zone of fire in an underserved niche. This is not just about expressing yourself or following your passion, it is equally about making money and serving the market. What he suggests is that you look to find a topic area that is not inundated with competitors and then fill that void.

"Find a niche," he says, and then "niche down some more. Niche until it hurts."

In JLD's case, that niche was not only a show where he interviewed entrepreneurs, but by "niching down," he realized that the market opportunity was in doing that show every day. He figured that "podcast listeners listen to podcasts," and as such, a daily show might strike a chord. People commute in their car every day, go to the gym and work out, and so on. If they liked podcasts, they might like a daily show.

When I asked John why he thought his show took off and has been such a success, he said, *"I solved one problem better than anyone else."* There was a market and need for a daily show for entrepreneurs. Who knew? John did. "I had to find a void that was not being filled in the podcast marketplace." He says, " I had to find a niche that I could dominate from day one, not because I was better than the competition, but because of the lack of competition."

John's zone of fire was a podcast.

What is yours?

WEBINARS

The last option available to you in this digital toolbox is no less powerful than the others, and in fact, in some ways may be the most powerful of them all.

Webinars can teach, inform, entertain, and influence. They can be heard live and/or recorded for replay later. They can consist of static slides, interactive video, livestreams, written words, colorful graphics, and all matters of visuals in between. Presentations can be made by a person or a team. Webinars can be hosted on your own website, or a site like ClickFunnels, or some third-party host.

The sheer variety and possibilities of webinars makes them a very potent option for a sonic business boom. Personally, while I have used all of the tools in this chapter, I have had the most success with webinars. I find them to be just a great way to connect with people, deliver valuable information, share my passion and expertise, be creative, and stand out, and I bet you would too.

> Good webinar platforms include ReadyTalk, GoToWebinar, Zoom, Zoho Meeting, WebinarJam, and ON24.

Yet the benefits of giving webinars go well beyond that. Here are some other benefits of webinars:

Webinars are engaging and interactive. A typical webinar might consist of 45 minutes of prepared slides and 15 minutes of Q&A. Other webinars can last for hours. This equals a winner on two fronts:

- First, where else do you get an audience's attention for an hour or more, especially online? That webinars can be so engaging is unique.
- The interactivity aspect of a webinar is also distinctive. People listen live and can ask questions live. You can poll your audience or solicit feedback in real time. You simply do not get that sort of live engagement with a video or podcast.

The content is substantive and valuable. Webinars provide real value to real people in real time.

They are brandtastic! From the start, the webinar presenter is the main attraction of the event. Additionally, slides can be branded with business logos and URLs.

They grow your list. Apropos of our earlier discussion, it is not insignificant that people have to register to watch either the live webinar or the taped recording. Those registrations can be added to your list.

Webinars attract a large global audience. A typical webinar might attract several hundred people from all over the country or all over the world. Some webinars attract tens of thousands of guests. Not only is it amazing to be able to speak to a worldwide audience, it is a privilege to get to do so. And especially with COVID-19 still on our brains, that you do not have to get on a plane or navigate airports or check into a hotel makes webinars even more attractive.

One wonders how someone like Don Draper might have fared in this collaborative, transparent, value-added, social media dominant, digital new world we live in. Having an impact was his thing, and so being on the right side of the digital divide is a given. It is not hard to imagine that, as he did at the end of *Mad Men*, Don might have had an epiphany, learned a few things, and would have gone on to be, say, a Facebook Live influencer who uses the Coca-Cola jingle he invented as his trademark bumper music.

BOOM YOUR BUSINESS BOTTOM LINE

▶ In this digital world, there is a marked difference between entrepreneurs who take advantage of the digital tools available and those who do not. Being on the right side of this digital divide is often the difference between boom and bust.

▶ There are many digital tools that you can use, but six stand out: an opt-in list, funnels, livestreaming videos, videos, podcasts, and webinars.

▶ Each tool has different benefits and drawbacks. The ones that are best for you are usually those with which you are viscerally most comfortable.

▶ Fortunes can be made by tapping into, mastering, and consistently using the right tool for your business and brand.

CHAPTER

GET 100,000 FOLLOWERS

Do not follow where the path may lead.
Go instead where there is no path
and leave a trail.
—Ralph Waldo Emerson

Picture this: You are in your swanky law office, you are young, smart, savvy, and successful. You have succeeded on every wrung of the ladder . . . but something is amiss.

That was the case not so long ago for Elma Beganovich. A graduate of Georgetown Law, Elma had interned on Capitol Hill, clerked with the Department of Justice, and at this point, had a busy securities law practice.

At that time (circa 2012), her sister Amra was in a similar position in her life and career. No less smart or successful, Amra had been an economics major at George Mason University, and then got her master's in economics from Schiller International University. She was, at this time of sisterly ennui, working as an economist for the World Bank.

So, yes, their careers up until that point were quite impressive, if a tad dry. But glamorous? No, not so much. That would change.

Today the sisters have more than 2 million social media followers and are, according to *Forbes*, the "epicenter of influence."

Not only that, but they also manage an exciting, in-high-demand digital marketing agency.

Indeed, their agency really is something to behold. A&E is a "marketing agency that uses strategies known to superstar influencers to make brands explode digitally." No mere boast, clients run the gamut from Bvlgari to Swarovski to Olay, Netflix, and Wells Fargo. Services include influencer marketing (naturally), media buying, social media management, PR, and SEO. Today, Amra and Elma travel the world on behalf of clients and rake in huge fees doing so.

No, not a bad gig, not at all. And certainly not boring.

This then begs the questions: How did they get from where they were to where they are (read on), and can you do the same? (Yes.)

> "**Problem:** Bvlgari wanted to showcase their jewelry, handbags, and other accessories while also promoting their new Bvlgari resorts. Their goal was to portray Bvlgari as a lifestyle brand and have influencers experience resorts.
>
> **Solution:** A&E contracted influencers to travel from United States to Bali, Dubai and Milan to style, photograph, and share Bvlgari jewelry, handbags and accessories. We traveled to the desert while in Dubai to produce an editorial for the Serpentine collection. In Milan, we produced an editorial for the diamond Serpentine jewelry.
>
> **Stats:** 4.7M+ followers targeted, 20 posts in total, 500,000+ in engaged audience"[1]

The smart, savvy sisters started their pivot by doing what entrepreneurs are often told to do, namely, something they loved. As they told me, they began their journey to social media stardom almost on a whim, and in their "spare time;" they started writing, blogging, taking photographs, and posting about their passions—travel, fashion, makeup, and the like.

But get this: When they began in 2012, blogs were not nearly as prevalent as they are today, so they had to code their own blog. Yes, you read that right. As they told Jeff Bulas on his website JeffBulas.com,

> Basically, what had happened is that Amra sat up one night all night and tried to figure out code. Tried to basically set up our first blog on Blogger. Blogger, as you probably remember, was kind of a competitor with WordPress. So she sat up that night and was kind of struggling with HTML, and CSS to customize our blog. [And] she did.

It didn't hurt that they seemed to have a sixth sense about what their audience would respond to. Within a couple of months, their eye-catching content was getting more than 100,000 visitors a month to their new blog. Needless to say, they quickly expanded onto various social media platforms, especially Instagram, where such visually striking images work so well.

Around this time, in the first year of their new venture, you could get Amra and Elma to tweet about you for $99.

Today, it is $20,000 per sponsored Instagram post and up.

There are several lessons to be learned from the tale of the sisters Beganovich, but insofar as creating an online following goes, a few jump to the top:

- Creating a large following is not simply about "popularity." Instead, in this social media–driven world we live in, deciding to generate a large online following is a strategic move that can yield enormous business benefits, including increased revenue and new, unique opportunities.
- Success is a matter of great content, yes, but just as important, great engagement. As Elma told me, "Having good content is not enough. You have to get people to notice it." How? You need to post it where your desired audience "can easily find it and share it."

Amra and Elma also suggest that you "follow the influencers you want to influence and give them a compliment or a shout out." If you tag your followers and influencers in your posts, they will be more likely to share your content. Their followers then will learn about you and can begin to follow you as well.

Now, it may be that you are not interested in taking the time (because it does take time) and putting in the energy (ditto) required to create a million followers. Fair enough (personally, I have 100,000 followers and that keeps me plenty busy). But a lot can be said for putting in the work to create a six-figure following. Having that kind of following goes far beyond an ego trip. It will:

- Enable a lot more potential customers to discover you and your business
- Position you as an expert or your brand as a brand
- Empower you to command significantly higher fees
- Give you influence

So, yes, getting from here to there is definitely worth the effort.

GAINING FOLLOWERS THE OLD-FASHIONED WAY

Back in the day, there was a famous commercial for a wealth management firm called Smith Barney. In a typical ad, an old, stuffy-looking British actor named John Houseman sat in an equally stuffy-looking restaurant and intoned:

> *Good investments don't walk up, bite you on the bottom and say, "We're here." Finding them takes good, old-fashioned hard work. Research. The kind they do at Smith Barney. Smith Barney is among a handful of firms singled out for their work in research. Smith Barney— they make money the old-fashioned way. They earn it.*

"They earn it" went on to be something of a catchphrase of the era, and it applies here, too. As with online traffic, there are essentially two ways to gain a large social media following—organic and paid.

The first, organic, apropos of Smith Barney, is indeed the old-fashioned way—you earn it. That is, by being visible, creating, posting, and sharing content, and by slowly but surely getting more well known, you can create an organic following. The typical advice given to people looking to increase their organic reach is to "be authentic," "create great content," and "post regularly."

And, while all of those are true and constitute good advice, it is also true that creating an organic following is usually an achingly slow process unless you catch lightening in a bottle. It can literally take years to go from a few dozen followers to a five-figure following, let alone a six-figure following (if ever). But this is how most people and businesses go about it—without a strategy, posting content ad hoc, adding their social handles to emails and their website, and hoping for the best.

Now, make no mistake about it, the old-fashioned way works, albeit usually in a methodical, herky-jerky way. There is nothing wrong with going about creating a following this way—most people do it—but just don't expect to generate the kind of income, recognition, and connections that can quickly move the needle.

And given that, it begs the question: Is attempting to grow your social following organically even worth the effort? There are pros and cons:

Pros
- It is basically free. Organic reach takes time but not money.
- It works. Slowly but surely.
- Sometimes it explodes. That is, on occasion people get lucky and write an article or post a video that goes viral, like, say, "The 'Five Guys' Fries Trick That Will Blow Your Mind (And Sales!)." The problem however is that being a "one-hit wonder" is not sustainable; it's a fluke. You might see a spike in followers for a quick bit, but that's it.

Cons

- It's usually haphazard. There is nothing strategic about posting irregularly and hoping for the best.
- It's not the most effective.
- It's usually very sloooow. Have I mentioned this yet?

As you might have guessed, I am advocating for the second method; that you be far more intentional when it comes to creating a large social media following. Using the paid strategy I outline here will be faster, far more effective, but also, yes, more expensive.

That is the price you have to pay, literally and figuratively.

GETTING 100,000 OR MORE FOLLOWERS, RIGHT NOW

As opposed to waiting for your organic following to eventually pay off, your other option is to be impatient and strategically prod the process. Doing so is a five-step process:

1. Microtarget your desired audience.
2. Pick the right platform(s).
3. Create and post content that users will share.
4. Pay to put that content in front of them.
5. Analyze and refine your results.

(Note: I first learned of this method after reading the book *One Million Followers: How I Built a Massive Social Following in 30 Days* by Brendan Kane. This is a great book, and I highly recommend it.)

1. Microtarget Your Desired Audience

Marketing used to be so much more difficult.

Pre-internet, a marketer had but a few big mass-media choices. TV, radio, newspapers, magazines, billboards—all were expensive and, in fact, for the small business, practically out of the question.

Intended to reach millions, mass media forced marketers to buy expensive ads that reached a mass audience, but only a tiny fraction of that audience would have any interest in what the marketer was selling. Buying ads that reached millions when you only needed to reach thousands (or hundreds) meant that advertising and marketing for the small business was practically cost-prohibitive.

For example, a local newspaper in a metropolitan area might be delivered to millions of homes. A small business wanting to spread the word via the paper would have to pay for all of those eyeballs, even though only a few would ever pay attention to the ad.

And that is why the internet generally, and Google specifically, revolutionized the advertising game.

Aside from search, Google's real innovation was the pay-per-click ad that showed up next to search results. By tying their ads to specific search results, *advertisers were able to microtarget their exact audience, and—even better—only pay for ads when someone clicked on them.*

Think about that.

Say you were selling coffee beans. Instead of buying an expensive newspaper ad that few people would ever notice (let alone act on), you could, instead, buy online ads from Google that would be seen only by people in your city who searched for coffee, and you would only pay for that ad once someone clicked on it (hence, pay-per-click).

Game, set, match.

That same microtargeting can allow you to very adroitly locate and reach the people most likely to like you, like your content, and follow you and/or your business. Microtargeting can and should be a game changer for you.

Here's how: You will need to create the type of engaging content that is discussed throughout this book and in the next section and then place that content via ads in front of your specific, desired, microtargeted audience. They will then find it, and find you.

We begin with the targeting, however, because once you know who it is you are trying to reach, creating the sort of content that speaks to them is much easier. For the Beganovich sisters, once they zeroed in on their audience of younger women who shared their passion for fashion and travel, creating the sort of dynamic, visual content that would resonate with them was much more obvious.

So, just who is it you want to target?

- What is their age?
- What is their gender?
- How much money do they make?
- Where do they live? Is your audience local, national, or international?
- Single, married, or divorced?
- What types of occupations do they have?
- What is their education level?
- What are their interests? This is key. Consider:
  - Where do they shop, online and off?
  - What brands do they like?
  - What do they read, watch, and listen to?
  - What are their recreational activities?

If you are seeking to reach folks in red states, your answers would be different than if you wanted to reach people in blue states. One is more rural, one more urban. They generally have different education levels, interests, values, and so on. Knowing— really knowing—who your audience is will ensure that you do not waste your precious time and money targeting folks who might have no interest in your message.

How do you figure out who your audience is and what they like? Homework. Start with your current customers. Poll them. Ask the above sorts of questions, and further, ask about your brand

and content. What do and don't they like about it? You can ask the same questions to people who are part of your e-newsletter opt-in list, or your current social following.

And remember, while you certainly have a good idea about who your audience is and what they like because they are, after all, your customers, your presumptions and assumptions can be wrong. That is why polling them is so important.

> Getting people to respond to a poll, survey, or questionnaire can be difficult. One way to generate responses is to incentivize them with a giveaway, freebie, or special deal.

Next, dive into Google Analytics for your website and Facebook Insights (if you have a business Facebook account). These advanced analytics can answer many of these sorts of questions.

The purpose of being able to target your best audience is multifold: First, as indicated, it will enable you to create content that speaks to them. These are the folks most likely to click, like, share, swipe, call, email, or whatever other action it is you seek. It also means that you will be able to create *lookalike audiences* for your Facebook or Google ads.

As indicated in the previous chapter, a lookalike audience is a group of people in a social network that has the same characteristics as your core audience. Both Facebook and Google allow you to target your content and ads to such a lookalike audience (in fact, Facebook invented lookalike audiences). As such, once you know your target group demographics, reaching similar people suddenly gets much easier.

Facebook can build a lookalike audience from customer lists, website visitors, page likes, locations, and other demographic details. Facebook recommends that you have an original audience of at least 1,000 in order to create a good lookalike audience.

Back in 2009, at the dawn of Twitter, I was asked by a reader if they "should Twitter?" (It really was the very early stages of the platform!) My unenlightened answer was an emphatic no:

> Yes, I know, Twitter is all the rage. Everyone is either
> tweeting or talking about it or following someone and
> so, yes, I get that Twitter is the flavor of the month. But
> know what else I know? Sometimes you don't want
> or don't need the flavor of the month; sometimes you
> need chocolate or vanilla. Sometimes newer isn't better.

Two important things happened as a result of that ignorant piece. First, that column became, up until that point, the most shared thing I had ever written, and not for good reasons. "This Strauss dude really doesn't get it!" was the general theme.

Second, I heard from a PR pro, Gini Dietrich (www .SpinSucks.com), who explained why I was wrong. The real value of getting followers, she said, is that it allows you to meet people you otherwise would not normally meet and therefore enables you to significantly grow your business in ways you can't anticipate.

In her case, the Great Recession had really hurt her business. Not knowing what else to do, she joined Twitter and began engaging with folks in her industry, meeting new people, getting followers, and forging new relationships. To her surprise, many of those people ended up hiring her. The result? As she gained more and more followers and connections, and as she ended up doing more and more deals, Gini's business *grew* by 21 percent that year.

2. Pick the Right Platform(s)

The different social media platforms have different audiences and engagement styles. The content you post on one likely is not the content that will work on others. The pithy tweet that gets retweeted would likely get lost on Facebook and be ignored on LinkedIn.

- Instagram is a visual medium requiring attractive, eye-catching visuals.
- Tweets are of course shorter, tighter.
- Facebook posts are longer. Visuals, video, and memes work well.
- LinkedIn lends itself to longer, more sober articles.
- YouTube (of course) requires videos.
- TikTok's micro-videos are shot on cell phones and last no more than 15 seconds.

Beyond that, the different platforms cater to different demographics (generally speaking). According to the Khoros.com 2021 Social Media Guide:

- Sixty-seven percent of people between ages 18 and 29 use Instagram.
- Roughly only 25 percent of Twitter's audience is 55 and older.
- The most active group on LinkedIn is aged 25 to 34.
- Everyone seems to use Facebook, including, surprisingly, 86 percent of people under 29.
- Thirty-seven percent of millennials binge watch YouTube daily.[2]
- Almost half of TikTok users are between 16 and 24. Fifty-six percent are male and 44 percent are female.

Seventy-three percent of Gen Z adults (born between 1997 and 2015) are active on Instagram, followed by Snapchat at 63 percent and YouTube at 62 percent.

Yet, whatever all of these statistics say, *the most important thing to consider when picking the platform or platforms where you will post is where your audience is.* Not what you like, not where you go, not where your pals hang out, but where your audience is. If they are on Twitter, then you need to be on Twitter, if they are on Instagram, then you need to post on Instagram.

3. Create and Post Content They Will Share

As Brendan Kane says in *One Million Followers*, "shareability is the most important metric when looking to grow quickly."

The reason for this, he says, is that having someone read and like your content is all well and good, but it is static. "It doesn't produce results. Someone who shares your content [however], is taking action."

Kane tells the story of magician Julius Dein, who got more than 15 million followers in 15 months. Dein says that he does not care about views when posting videos. "I don't care if the videos got two million views on Facebook. I care about how many shares it has because if it's got a lot of shares that means it's exponential."

How to Get Retweeted

Guy Kawasaki (1.4 million Twitter followers) notes that 70 percent of retweets contain links. In addition he says, "The word 'you' is the most likely word to occur in retweets compared to tweets, and the least retweetable words include 'going,' 'watching,' 'work,' 'home,' 'well,' and 'tired.'"

—GuyKawasaki.com

Much of the advice given previously in Chapter 8, "Creating Clickable Content," applies equally here. Sharable content begins with a good headline. This is what draws them in. But a killer headline is not nearly enough. If the content is not great, if it does not deliver on the promise of the headline, people will not share it. Therefore, it also needs to connect quickly. Brendan Kane says that you only have "a second (or three max) to hook someone and grab their interest."

Beyond that, sharable content connects to people on an emotional, visceral level. Whether that emotion is joy, sorrow, anger, or laughter, once they feel something they are far more inclined to share it. It also uses images or video. Social media stars know that using images and video can dramatically increase the number of shares.

And finally, sharable content is content that in some way helps the people who are sharing it. Think about it: By sharing your content, they are giving it their stamp of approval. They are putting their word behind it and telling the world, "Hey, check it out, I think this is cool, and I bet you will too." They get value by sharing your great content.

In that sense, sharing your content is the "word of mouth" in the digital age. Word of mouth, as we all know, is the ultimate form of marketing—that personal stamp of approval can't be beat. In the world of social media, word of mouth means the sharing of content. And why would someone give their stamp of approval? Because your content is that good, that interesting, that valuable.

Offer them that, and they will want to spread the word by co-branding with you.

4. Pay to Put That Content in Front of Them

So you have microtargeted your ideal audience and have begun to create content that you think they will like and respond to. Now they have to see it and share it if you want your following to grow exponentially. As mentioned, the fastest way to do that is to advertise it.

Every social media platform supports some sort of advertising, whether it is sponsored tweets or getting Facebook Likes or a YouTube ad. Your job is to decide which one best fits your tribe, learn its advertising platform and post your content, microtargeted to your desired audience. Do this again and again, with lots of content.

For the sake of discussion, let's look at Facebook.

When you go to Facebook's advertising platform, you are given several choices for the type of advertising result you want to get. You can boost a post, get more likes, promote your page, get more subscribers, or get more website visitors.

Two in particular are most important for this discussion: boosting posts and buying more page likes. Both will allow you to put your ad and content in front of your desired target market with the intention of having them like your page, share your content, or follow you.

There is one other highly effective—and definitely less expensive—ways to quickly get your name, brand, business, and content in font of people: Target your ads toward people in developing, English-speaking countries. On Facebook, targeting your posts and ads and acquiring followers in India, for example, is much less expensive than doing the same in the United States. Whereas an American follower on Facebook might cost a dime, one in India can cost a penny. But even so, those Indian followers have all of the attributes you want in a follower: They are educated, English speaking, digitally savvy, and they engage online.

Or what about YouTube? YouTube is now available in more than 100 countries, in 80 languages, and in fact, 89 percent of YouTube users come from outside the United States.[3] Bottom line: getting foreign followers should be neither difficult nor costly.

5. Analyze and Refine Your Results

This last step is critical. There will be a learning curve using this system. Figuring out what sort of content resonates and which strategies work best takes time and effort. The different ad platforms take a while to master.

That is why you have to test.

You should test different types of content on different platforms. Test headlines. Test different audiences. Test posting on different days and different times. Especially at the beginning of this venture, create, post, share, and advertise many different types of content.

After some trial and error, you will discover what works best, that is, what is shared the most and what sort of content and ads generate the most followers and bang for your buck.

Once you learn that, congrats, you are on your way to six figures.

BOOM YOUR BUSINESS BOTTOM LINE

▶ There are two ways to get a huge social media following: the slow way and the fast way.

▶ While the slow way is a lot more affordable, it is also time-consuming and somewhat tedious. It is a matter of posting quality content on social sites again and again . . . and again.

▶ While the fast way does cost money, it is often worth it because the benefits of a huge social following are usually monetary in nature.

▶ Creating that following the fast way is a five-step process: (1) Microtarget your desired audience. (2) Pick the right platform(s). (3) Create and post content that people will share. (4) Put that content in front of them via advertising. (5) Analyze and refine your results.

▶ Boom!

CHAPTER

MARKETPLACE MANIA

What's dangerous is not to evolve.

—Jeff Bezos

Sure, a large social following is great, but even still, I have a question for you: **Do you shop on Amazon?** Of course you do. I do too. We all do.

And that's the point.

If the whole world is shopping on Amazon.com, if the site gets almost 10 million visitors *a day*, and if you are looking to grow, then it should make sense that, aside from buying on Amazon, you should sell there, too. Right?

Amazon is, quite frankly, a small business boom factory.

- Annual sales by all Amazon third-party sellers during the otherwise *annus horribilis* of 2020 grew from an average of $100,000 a year to $160,000.[1]
- More than 15,000 small and medium businesses surpassed $1 million in sales on Amazon in 2019.[2]
- Fifty-five percent of consumers *begin* their online shopping search on Amazon.[3]

According to Nicholas Denissen, VP of small business at Amazon, "More than half of the items sold in Amazon's stores are from small and medium-sized businesses, so our success is deeply tied to their success."

THE ONLINE MARKETPLACE BOOM

Of course, Amazon is not the only marketplace game in town. There are many, many different online marketplaces that you can tap into. These include Facebook Marketplace, eBay, Walmart, and Etsy.

Also, aside from these big-name, branded sites, there are all sorts of lesser-known but by no means small, niche sites. Fruugo .us features inexpensive items sold globally: "Using our translation technology we translate your products into 28 languages." Bonanza.com offers "everything but the ordinary." And Chewy .com is all things pets.

Every and any one of these sites has the potential to rock your business world.

The Logic of the Marketplace

While sites like Amazon and Walmart are known for being very affordable places to buy goods sold by those companies, they also promote and encourage third-party sales on their platforms. This allows small businesses to access the millions of consumers who turn to these platforms first when shopping. You get the reach of Amazon and Walmart without the cost of having to advertise like Amazon and Walmart. Sweet!

According to eMarketer, e-commerce sales grew, year-over-year, by an astounding 28 percent in 2017, by 23 percent in 2018, and by 20.7 percent in 2019. Not surprisingly, due to COVID-19, e-commerce sales exploded in 2020, jumping by a whopping 77 percent, according to a report by Adobe. "According to our data, it would've taken between 4 and 6 years to get to the levels that we saw [at the height of the pandemic.]"[4]

The Benefits of Selling on Online Marketplaces

Given the explosive growth of e-commerce generally over the past decade, and since 2020 in particular, the opportunity for third-party sellers online is enormous. In addition to this tremendous growth, the potential for success is even higher due to two additional factors.

1. **Built-in audiences.** All of these major online retail marketplaces have ginormous built-in audiences who regularly rely on these sites for their shopping. Between Amazon, Walmart, and eBay alone, *there are close to a half a billion monthly visitors.*

2. **Ease of use.** If you are new to selling online this way, have no fear. These marketplaces want you to succeed, because when you succeed, they succeed. As such, they work to make it very easy for their small business partners to get started, sell, and fulfill orders. The learning curve is substantially decreased due to the many tutorials, tips, tools, and various programs they offer.

And, even if you already have some e-commerce experience, you are likely leaving money on the table if you are not also selling on a marketplace. Why? Because e-buyers have become accustomed to comparison shopping. As such, if they only find your wares on your own e-commerce site, it is very possible that they are using your site to look, learn, and compare, but not necessarily to buy . . . and that is just plain wrong!

However, if your products can be found not only on your own site, but on these marketplace platforms as well, there is a much greater likelihood for making extra sales given that more people, and more people ready to buy, will be seeing your stuff in more places.

Make sense?

MARKETPLACE SUCCESS SECRETS

Let's begin by acknowledging that when it comes to selling on these platforms, there is good news and bad news. The good news is that there are millions of people shopping on these sites. The bad news is there are millions of sellers trying to sell to them too.

Fortunately, there are a few strategies that you can adopt from the get-go that will help you in the long run:

Do your homework. Whatever platform you choose, learn it, live it, love it. As mentioned, they want to help you succeed, but—to paraphrase Jerry Maguire—you have to help them help you. All of those tools are worthless if you don't learn and use them.

Offer great products, photographs, descriptions, and headlines. This, of course, is e-commerce 101, but it bears repeating, especially if you are new to marketplace selling.

Online, attention spans are short. You only have—literally—a few seconds to impress people once they find your online store. Given that, your products and photos have to be top-notch, and your product descriptions have to be concise and clever.

Theo Prodromitis is the CEO of Spa Destinations, a seller of natural sponges, loofas, and other products designed to create an in-home spa experience. Spa Destinations started as a third-party seller on Amazon in 2014. In 2020, its Amazon sales topped $3 million.

How did they do it? I asked Theo:

Q: Theo, your success is impressive, but isn't it pretty difficult to get found on Amazon?

A: No, not really. The system is designed to be customer-centric, so if you sell quality items and get good reviews, you get found.

Q: OK, but isn't Amazon just for people looking for bargains?

A: Absolutely not. Amazon shoppers are quite sophisticated, so really, high-quality products like the ones we sell do great.

Q: Let me ask about new sellers. If someone reading this book would like to get started selling on Amazon, what advice do you have?

A: First, start small, test, and see what works. Try selling 5 to 10 items to start. Second, make sure, as I said, that you sell quality goods.

Also, and this is really important—you have to become an expert at selling on Amazon. Learn how to list, learn Amazon's logistics, learn about Fulfillment by Amazon ["FBA"—you sell it, Amazon ships it]. Also, learn how to tell the story of your products and business in your listings. Amazon makes this really easy.

Q: How?

A: Amazon's seller's tools are amazing. They give you access to the world's best analytics, marketers, marketplaces, experts, and so on. Incredible insight is available, but you have to access it and use it. One key to success, then, is to take the time and make the effort to learn and use these tools. Do your homework, read the articles Amazon has on the site, watch the videos, and so on.

Amazon and its experts want to help you succeed. They will train you, teach you how to be customer-centric, and so on.

Q: What tools do you like best?

A: One we really like is called Brand Dashboard. It helps you create, market, and manage your brand and business. The

analytics are amazing, and it also helps you identify and
protect your brand from copycats. Another one we like is
Launchpad.

Q: Anything else you would like to add?

A: It doesn't cost a lot to get started. We don't even do a lot
of advertising on the site. Look at your dashboard and see
what is selling. The system then suggests ads. We use
those ads, sales go up, and then we go back to organic.
Amazon really is a marketer's dream.

Use keywords. Until you get more established (and actually,
even after you do), marketplace sales are often a function
of search results. You need to learn the search queries and
keywords most often used by buyers when they log on to
Amazon or eBay or wherever and search for something
related to your business.

Say, for example, that you sell hoodies. Do potential
customers search for "hoodies" or "sweatshirts" or "zipped
sweatshirts" or what? Whatever the answer, those terms need
to be part of the descriptions of your products, as well as in
your product titles and tags.

If they search "hooded sweatshirts" and your listing only
mentions "hoodies," either they won't find you or they won't
choose you.

Offer free shipping. Amazon created a bit of a monster with
Prime as customers have come to expect free shipping, and
within a few days to boot. You will, therefore, need to build
the cost of shipping into your pricing.

On all of these sites, sellers typically offer a variety of
shipping options (aside from free.) Free is usually slower
(because they use USPS for this). That said, people will pay
more for faster delivery, so offer this too.

Advertise. It is not always possible to get to the top of organic search results on these sites, but even so, you can buy your way there.

Really? Yes.

By advertising on a site, your products can show up on the first page of a search result as a "featured" or "sponsored" product. In fact, the default Amazon search displays featured products first.

The other good thing about using Amazon advertising is that it can take the guesswork out of your keyword strategy. According to blog.Hubspot.com,

> *Amazon Sponsored Products uses keywords to trigger your ads. "Automatic targeting" allows Amazon to choose your keywords for you and is often the right choice for new advertisers. You can also choose manual targeting where you pick your own keywords.*

QUICK-START GUIDE TO AMAZON, EBAY, WALMART, ETSY, AND FACEBOOK MARKETPLACE

Each of the major online sellers have their own pros and cons, rules and requirements.

Amazon

I have mentioned Amazon a lot in this chapter because, well, not highlighting it would be like writing about big mountains and failing to mention Mt. Everest. Amazon is the Mt. Everest of e-commerce marketplace sales.

Aside from its roughly 10 million monthly users, Amazon also boasts 100 million Prime members who spend an average of $1,400 a year there. Amazon has been offering virtual shelf space to small businesses since 2000, and the stats don't lie:

- More than a half a million small and medium-sized businesses (SMB) in the United States sell on the platform.
- These SMBs account for more than half of everything sold on the site.

Given that small businesses are in fact so important to Amazon, it should not be surprising that the company puts a lot into helping their small business partners succeed. For just one example, in 2020, Amazon invested $18 billion in logistics, tools, services, and programs to bolster the growth of its small business selling partners.

Case Study

Based in Provo, Utah, Rocco & Roxie Supply Co. is a family-owned pet supply business that launched on Amazon with about 10 products. Today they sell more than 50, and Fulfillment by Amazon handles the storage, packing, shipping, and customer service side of the business.

This arrangement allows the company—which now has eight full-time staffers—to focus on sales. And it has worked, big-time. One example—their top-selling product is an odor and stain eliminator that has sold more than a million units on Amazon.

Says co-owner Morgan Magleby, Rocco & Roxie is "a true Amazon success story. We have to pinch ourselves sometimes, we've been so blown away with how well these products have been received."[5]

When selling on any of these sorts of sites, you will, needless to say, have to pay fees. The fees you pay depend on what sort of selling plan you choose. Individual sellers on Amazon have no monthly fees and are charged $.99 per item sold. Closing fees vary. Professional sellers presently pay a $39.95 monthly fee, as well as referral fees and closing fees.

The process of getting started is simple:

- Create a seller account and choose your plan.
- Upload your products, pictures, and descriptions.
- Start selling, and possibly, advertising.

eBay

eBay has the distinction of being the first ever online marketplace. It began in 1995 when founder Pierre Omidyar launched Auction-Web, a site "dedicated to bringing together buyers and sellers in an honest and open marketplace."

Canadian Mark Fraser purchased the first item that Pierre Omidyar listed on the site in 1995—a broken laser pointer.[6]

AuctionWeb took off immediately and sold more than $7 million worth of goods in less than a year. In 1997, a program that would become a fundamental part of eBay was introduced—seller feedback, allowing buyers to rate sellers. This is another eBay first, as seller feedback, so ubiquitous now, was a novel idea back then. But it is critical to the eBay experience, and you need to keep that in mind if you go this route.

In September of 1997, AuctionWeb officially changed its name to eBay. (Pierre Omidyar had been living in an area in Northern California called "the south bay." The name eBay was a takeoff on that, standing for "electronic bay.")

As eBay grew, it became clear that Omidyar had really tapped into something. Thousands of sellers flocked to the site, and so to help them, eBay launched eBay University in 2000, designed to teach users how to become "master sellers." eBay University still teaches courses around the world.

Today, eBay is a global brand with 168 million active users generating almost $100 billion in annual sales. Whereas eBay began as both a site to sell used goods and as an auction site, today everything is sold there—from vintage Rolex watches to brand-new cars, and regular sales far outnumber auction sales.

How big and busy is eBay? It boasts 2 billion transactions a day.

---

eBay Facts

- In 2002, the private town of Bridgeville, California, was sold on eBay for $700,000.
- The most expensive item ever sold on eBay was a 405-foot yacht for $168 million.
- In 2004, someone sold an insect that had been encased in amber some 50 million years ago. It turned out that the insect was a species theretofore unknown, and the scientist who bought it tried unsuccessfully to name it after the site—*Mindarus ebayici*.

Getting started on eBay is very easy. Initially, it is a two-step process. First, you need to *list it*. Have a product, write a description, add pictures, price it competitively, and set a fair shipping price. *Next, you need to sell it.* Using "My eBay," you can manage your listings in one place. It allows you to track what you sell, send and receive emails, view bids, and more. The eBay mobile app does much the same thing.

If you are going to be selling a lot on eBay long-term, there are essentially four fees of which to be aware:

- Listing fees, also called "Insertion Fees." You can sell 200 items for free per month, and then it's 35 cents per item after that.
- Selling fees, also called "Final Value Fees." This is a fee on the total final sale, usually 10 percent.
- Listing upgrades, for things like bigger pictures, international site visibility, and more.
- Specialty fees, in some categories, for things like car sales and real estate.

Walmart

Walmart.com was launched in 2000 and now has almost 400 million online shoppers. While the dot-com part of the retail giant was admittedly slow to pick up steam, a change in focus in the past few years has enabled it to really become a player in the online marketplace world. A previous focus on books, electronics, and toys has now given way to an emphasis on "everyday essential items," apparel, and fresh food. As a result, Walmart's e-commerce sales grew by 43 percent in 2018.

Unfortunately, unlike Amazon and eBay, you cannot simply sign up and sell on Walmart.com. You must apply and be invited, and Walmart is known for having a fairly strict approval process. You need to be a proven, reputable seller of quality products at competitive prices to make it into this club.

To apply, go to https://marketplace.walmart.com.

Etsy

Etsy is a relative newcomer to the online marketplace world, but by being unique and different, it distinguished itself from the beginning. Etsy is *the* go-to marketplace for buying and selling handcrafted goods.

There are plenty of great reasons to consider selling on Etsy:

- **Qualified leads.** People go to Etsy because they are looking for handcrafted goods. If that is what you sell, these customers are your people.
- **Teammates.** Etsy sellers can team up with other Etsy sellers in collective stores. This way, you can take time off when needed, and also network with similarly minded creatives.
- **Wholesale sales.** Etsy Wholesale gives you the opportunity to access and sell to bigger wholesale clients, and you know, selling to bigger clients is a boomtastic idea.
- **Ease.** Selling on Etsy is uniform and easy. Fees are simple, and the marketing tools makes it easy to launch promotions and offer coupon codes to customers.

As an artist and solopreneur, I have a lot of balls to juggle in my business. I also have a lot of options about how and where I choose to build my business. Etsy has proven to be a great addition to my product and marketing mix. I considered building e-commerce into my own website but decided I didn't want to spend the time and money it would take to build, let alone to attract, a customer base.

Etsy is a great site for creative people who want to focus on what they are best at—creating. Etsy provides the platform and, most important, the web traffic of customers I would never be able to attract on my own. While I do need to adapt to their changing fees, algorithms, and policies from time to time, I still believe the trade-offs are more than worth it.

—**Tara Reed,** etsy.com/shop/TaraReedDesigns

Facebook Marketplace

If Facebook has entered into a new arena, you know it has to be hot. So, yes, marketplaces are hot. Needless to say, with its monthly

800 million visitors, Facebook became a big player in the marketplace world almost upon launch in 2016.

Needless to say, the obvious first reason to choose to sell here is that Facebook is, well, Facebook. Millions of people are on the site every day, and they stay for hours at a time. But the reasons go beyond that.

- **Posting is easy.** Upload a product and photo, write a description, and post away.
- **Mobile optimized.** Facebook's Marketplace is easily seen on mobile, the preferred way for many to access Facebook now.
- **Locally focused.** Facebook will post your items to people in your area automatically.
- **Easy interaction.** Using Facebook Messenger, interacting with customers is a breeze, and very useful.
- **No fees.** Yes, that's right. No fees.

Have I convinced you yet? Selling your products online on a marketplace is smart business.

But what's that you say? You sell services and not products? No worries, your pal Steve has you covered. Read the next chapter!

BOOM YOUR BUSINESS BOTTOM LINE

▶ E-commerce is now not just a matter of selling on your own website. Marketplaces like Facebook Marketplace, eBay, Walmart, and Etsy have revolutionized online selling.

▶ Even if you already do e-commerce on your own, you are likely leaving money on the table if you are not also selling on a marketplace.

▶ Yes, there is a lot of competition selling on sites like these; that is their promise and peril. The good news is that these sites *want you to succeed* and have created a plethora of tools to help you do so.

▶ Getting started is really just a matter of getting started. Pick a site that fits your business and brand and jump into the deep end.

PART III

THE MILLIONAIRE SOLOPRENEUR

We are now in an age where the self-employed one-person business can generate a seven-figure income. Find out how.

CHAPTER

FREELANCE FORTUNES

The only people who get paid enough, get paid what they're worth, are people who don't follow the instruction book, who are innovative, who work without a map.
—Seth Godin

One of the greatest things that has come along because of the internet is the advent of online platforms that connect freelancers and other creatives with people looking to hire such people. On sites like Upwork, Freelancer, Fiverr, and Guru, you can find talent in an amazing array of categories:

1. Graphic artists, web designers, app developers
2. Writers, bloggers, videographers, photographers
3. Marketing specialists, sales pros, virtual assistants
4. Even legal and other professional help

In fact, Freelancer.com says that its freelancers have done work in—get ready for it—more than 1,800 different categories.

When I needed to update one of my sites, I knew that despite my lack of expertise in web design, I would still be able to find someone on one of these sites who could help me. And I did. Abby Woods of Iconik Web (Iconikweb.com) gave me a great bid and did fantastic work. I expected that given my past experience with Upwork (the site where I found Abby) and her reputation and experience.

What I didn't expect was that she would still be working with me some seven years later.

So, yes, the opportunity to grow your freelance business on sites like these is very real indeed.

LEVELING THE PLAYING FIELD

People go into business for all sorts of reasons. It might be because they longed to be their own boss, or had a rockstar idea, or had a passion for, say, graphic design. But just because someone is a great graphic designer, it does not mean he is a great marketer.

In fact, he probably is not.

So, in this hypothetical world, a lot would have to go right for our graphic designer to get a gig. He would have to not only be a great artist and graphic designer, and have a crackerjack website, but he would also have to be a heck of a marketer and salesperson. He would also have to hope that people who needed his services would find his site, like it, find his portfolio, like it too, and contact him. He would then hope to close the sale.

The problem is, hope, as they say, is not a strategy.

That's why the advent of online freelance marketplaces like the ones mentioned is so revolutionary for the freelancer who sells services (as opposed to products.) In one place, you can find gigs, bid on them, communicate with clients, and get paid.

The solopreneur doesn't have to be so solo anymore. And, if you do it right, these platforms can really help you explode your freelance business.

Unfortunately, the opposite is also true—if you do it wrong, you can easily get lost amongst all of the competition. And make no mistake about it, there is *a lot* of competition. *Freelancer says that it has more than 48 million users and over 19 million jobs posted.*

*How much money can you make on Upwork? Successful freelancers on Upwork can earn **$100 to $175 per hour**, and sometimes more. It's common to see freelancers with lifetime earnings of $250,000, $500,000, and occasionally higher.*
—CareerSidekick.com

So let's do it right. Here's how:

THE TOP FIVE FREELANCE SITES

I think we can all agree that COVID-19 was good for nothing.

Well, almost nothing.

One of few the silver linings of the pandemic from the perspective of the solopreneur is that demand for freelance services shot up dramatically. Indeed, because of COVID-19, the whole world was forced to work online, and with everyone suddenly more reliant on the internet than ever before, the number of online projects offered shot through the roof. Freelancer, for example, says that they saw an uptick of around 50 percent in gigs offered in 2020, and that surge has continued.

There are a lot more than five sites where you can bid on gigs. But who wants to try out 20 different sites to see which one works best? Not us! Here then are the top ones, ranked by reputation, number of gigs available, quality of those gigs, and earning potential. (Note: All of these sites are good and so this list is not in order of "best to worst." They all have strengths and different things to offer.)

Upwork

Upwork was originally called Elance, and I must confess that I am partial to this site for two reasons. First, when I launched my site TheSelfEmployed, Elance was a founding sponsor (it actually *paid me* to help me get my site built, but that's a story for a different chapter). Second, as mentioned, I found my trusty sidekick Abby there. In the years since, I have had a lot of success posting gigs on

Upwork (though not looking for them), and so I know it is a great choice.

The good news is also the bad news when it comes to Upwork. Because the site is so popular, it has millions of listings—and millions of freelancers looking at those listings. Given that the way most projects on the site work is that freelancers bid against each other on proposed projects, there can be a fairly intense competition that drives down fees on Upwork. *On the other hand, price is only one consideration when people list projects on the site; they are often looking for the best, not the cheapest.*

As with most of these sites, you will have to pay a fee to Upwork for each gig. Current fees break down this way:

- Twenty percent for the first $500 billed with the client
- Ten percent for lifetime billings with the same client between $500.01 and $10,000
- Five percent for lifetime billings with that client exceeding $10,000

The quality of the work you can find on Upwork is pretty impressive, with many corporate clients looking for help with both one-time and long-term projects.

Freelancer

Freelancer and Upwork are probably the two oldest, and definitely the two largest, freelance gig sites on the Internet (although Upwork looks to be larger). The gigs on Upwork tend to be of better quality than those found on Freelancer (that is, they seem to pay better). The fees paid to the platform are similar to Upwork, with a percentage of income generated on the site going to the host.

Here's how it works: Companies and individuals post engagements on Freelancer, and then freelancers browse the listings, see the gigs and budgets, and then bid on the project. Whatever your specialty—be it making videos, blogging, research, being a virtual assistant, social media marketing, sales, or whatever—a site like Freelancer offers you an opportunity to find consistent work.

The challenge is that there is often a race to the bottom in terms of price. Free market capitalism being what it is, and given Freelancer's global footprint, there is intense pressure on this site to bid low to win projects, especially as you are competing with people in other parts of the world whose standard of living and corresponding wages are far below those in the West.

> Freelancing really has gone global, with an estimated 90 million freelancers working worldwide. Freelancer in particular caters to this global market, translating projects into dozens of languages, and thereby allowing freelancers from around the globe to find and get gigs.

Toptal

No low-bid competitions here. While Toptal is similar to Upwork and Freelancer, the difference is significant: Toptal has a very rigorous screening process and only accepts the top 3 percent of all freelancer applicants. As they say on the site, "Toptal is an exclusive network of the world's top talent in business, design, and technology. We provide access to top companies, a community of experts, and resources that can help accelerate your career."

It follows then that given that the quality of the freelancers on the site is the top, the quality of the gigs offered here is equally impressive. If you can get accepted, the opportunity to make significant amounts of money on Toptal is very real.

Beyond their brilliant technical capabilities, Toptalers are also screened on their soft skills including attitude, ethical values, energy, education, and English proficiency. We want to ensure they're amazing teammates, not just amazing workers.

—Toptal.com

Fiverr

Fiverr completely flips the script. Instead of people listing projects and independent contractors bidding on those projects, on Fiverr, freelancers list their expertise and products and buyers search for the freelancer who best fits their need. Fees paid to Fiverr are uniform—20 percent of every sale goes to the house.

As the name indicates, Fiverr is a site that rewards low prices. While originally gigs were listed for $5 each (a "fiver"), projects pay more now, but maybe not a whole lot more. Fiverr says that these days, gigs range from $5 to $10,000.

Fiverr seems to work best for freelancers who can quickly crank out a product time and again—whiteboard videos, voice-overs, photo manipulation, and so on. As such, it is best seen as a side hustle adjunct as opposed to a place like Toptal, where real money can be made.

SolidGigs

Finally, SolidGigs is another site that turns the traditional bid-on-a-gig model upside down, and I like it. One of the hassles of the other sites is that it takes quite a bit of time to search and find the right gigs to bid on.

SolidGigs fixes that.

On this site, you select the types of jobs you are best suited for, and then the team at SolidGigs does the searching for you. Each week they will send you a list of freelance jobs they have found (they peruse other sites listing gigs) that are, they say, the "top 1–2% of freelancing gigs." In exchange, you pay them a flat monthly fee of $19.

As the whole point of SolidGigs is that they search and send only the best projects that fit your designated criteria, the quality of projects you can get here is really quite good. That said, because this site is considerably smaller than the others on this list, the quantity of work you can expect to see is less.

QUICK-START GUIDE

Generally speaking, the actual process of getting started on one of these sites is simple:

1. **Create a profile.** Go to the site (or sites) and select your skills. You will list your experience and expertise, upload a photo, and post your bio.
2. **Browse jobs.** There are gigs for every skill level. Use the search engine and filters to find projects for your level and interests.
3. **Bid.** Once you find a project that is a good fit, pitch yourself. Explain why you are the best person for the job. Make your fee competitive, but don't give away the store.
4. **Work.** Do your best. Get great feedback. Get hired again. Rinse and repeat.

Of course, in reality, it is not nearly as basic as following a four-step process; that is just an overview. There are significant gaps between browsing, bidding, working, and repeating.

So let's fill in those gaps.

Start Small

A wise man I know has a saying that is quite apropos. He often said that (with apologies to Mama Gump), "Life is like a jar of pickles."

Think about a pickle jar. When you first open it, they are all jammed in there, right? Getting the first pickle out of the jar is difficult. But after you do, after you coerce that first one out, what happens? All of the rest of the pickles come out very easily. *So the challenge and the trick is to get that first pickle out of the jar.*

So too here. You need to get that first gig pickle out of the jar because after that, all of the other gigs will come much easier. After the first, you will have work to share, seller feedback to show, a presence on the site.

So, how do you get your first pickle—err, gig—on Upwork or Freelancer or wherever? Start small. On any of these sites, the bottom-rung gigs are indeed small: $50 maybe. And that's OK. There is little risk for a client when hiring someone new for $50, so the competition for such gigs is quite low. That means that the chance of you getting the first pickle out is quite high.

Get Feedback

Undoubtedly, $50 or $100 for whatever the project is, is going to be below either your normal rate or what you are really worth. That's fine. That's the point. The key is twofold:

1. To do great work, and thereby
2. To be able to get great feedback on the site about you, your mad skills, and your work ethic.

This is the key, the real first pickle. Once you can post positive feedback on your profile, you become a much more viable commodity.

It's like word of mouth. Having a customer on the site sing your praises tells other customers that you can be trusted and do good work.

My first father was the best entrepreneur I ever knew. He and his partner grew a single carpet store in Los Angeles into the biggest carpet chain in California at the time. Dad was in charge of marketing, and he used it all: TV ads, Sunday inserts, parking lot sales, grand openings, the whole enchilada.

After 20 years, however, it all got too big and Dad sold out and started over again with a single store, a giant carpet warehouse that also became very successful. But this time, Dad didn't buy expensive TV ads or use gimmicky sidewalk sales to drive traffic. Instead, he did only one thing: When people would walk into Carpet World, they would immediately see a giant banner hanging in the middle of the store.

"Our word-of-mouth advertising starts with you!"

What dad learned over the course of his career is that no amount of slick banner ads or billboards or half-off sales held a candle to word-of-mouth advertising.

The other advantage of starting small is that it will help you learn how the platform works while also allowing you to begin to forge relationships with the customers who are hiring. You never know what leads to what. That little one-off could become an ongoing, long-term gig.

Just ask Abby!

Maximize Your Profile

The first thing potential clients look at on these sites is your profile. So you need to maximize and optimize yours:

- **Fill out all fields and forms.**
- **Have a great job title.** Clients quickly peruse the different contractors on these sites, so you need to have a catchy, great title for your bio. Test different ones to see which words get you more views.
- **Write a great bio.** Be sure to read the bios of similar, highly rated freelancers and see how they write their bios. That's your template.
- **List your hourly rate.** Aside from your profile title, your hourly rate is the other thing that drives page views. You may be tempted to list a low hourly rate because that will indeed increase page views, but be forewarned, people looking for the lowest bidder may not be the best clients. And ask yourself: Do you want to be known as "the low-cost leader"?

Insider Tip

If you are new to these sites and want to get chosen, consider offering a skill few others on the site offer. There was once a bestselling small business book called *Niche and Grow Rich*, and that's the idea, especially in the beginning. Offer the crowd a niche skill.

Yes, that may seem challenging, but it is also doable. Say that you are a digital marketer. Sure, plenty of people know how to advertise on Facebook, but how many know how to market on TikTok? Learn that skill and highlight it on your profile. That will help you stand out from the crowd.

Apply for Gigs

On these sites, you get hired in one of two ways. Either people find you and request your services (because you have the right background and/or a lot of positive feedback), or you search and find gigs listed and you bid on them. The second way is what we are talking about here.

You have created business proposals previously, and whatever worked there will likely work here. Bottom line: *Your proposal needs to stand out.* Here's how:

Make it personal. Don't use a template when writing to a potential client. Instead, write to the person, use their name, and to the extent you can do a bit of research and learn about their business, do so.

Don't sell, help. No one likes a hard sell, so don't do that. Instead, show customers how you can assist them. Be curious. Ask questions. Offer solutions.

Don't be boring. Rote, by-the-numbers proposals or inquiries will get glossed over, and deservedly so. However you do it, be creative and stand out.

Get invited to the party. After a while, after you have completed several projects and have reviews and a reputation, you will begin to get invited to bid on projects. That's the ticket. Potential clients will have seen your profile and work and reputation and reviews and will have decided that you just might fit the bill.

Close the Deal

It is difficult to say which happened faster—the spread of COVID-19 or the spread of Zoom; you have to admit that it's a pretty close call. The point being, Zoom calls became all the rage during the pandemic, and they are not going away anytime soon. You very well may have to have to sell yourself on a Zoom call with your potential client.

We have all had job interviews, both good and bad, so you know the drill. Ask questions about the client, ask about his or her business, ask about the project, ask about expectations. Explain why you are the best person for the job. Crack a joke.

Finally, it helps to not be too anxious. Play a little hard to get. Explain that you are pretty busy right now, but because this gig sounds so interesting, you will be happy to make room for it.

"YOU WON'T GET RICH BILLING BY THE HOUR"

There are two inherent obstacles to creating a business boom when working on sites like Upwork and Fiverr: your number of billable hours in a year and your per-hour billing rate.

Consider the first issue—the number of hours available when you bill by the hour.

Let's say your goal is to make $250,000 next year. If you work 50 weeks a year, you need to earn $5,000 a week, or $1,000 a day, to hit that goal. Realistically, you can expect to work about, say, six billable hours a day (which would take at least eight actual hours). To bill $5,000 would therefore require you charge about $170 an hour, and that bumps up against the second issue, namely, the going per-hour billable rate.

So, even if you can somehow charge $170 an hour (and a lot of independent contractors cannot), you would also need to work your tail off, every day, five days a week, week after week if you want to reach your goal.

Possible? Possibly, but not for most self-employed people, and probably not consistently. What does that mean then? An old business truism applies here: *You won't get rich billing by the hour.*

Here are two very viable alternatives:

1. **Bill by the project.** Bigger projects lead to bigger paydays, better work, less time, and often, happier clients. Juggling a few big projects is also easier than managing a lot of small gigs that pay less.

   It's also financially smart in that if you are able to complete the project in less time than you would have been able to billing by the hour, then you will make more. The delta between the two is profit.

   Yes, it will take time to build up a portfolio that is impressive enough that you will be able to bid on bigger gigs, but it's worth it.

2. **Become a gig entrepreneur.** Great entrepreneurs make money, even on days when they do not work.

   How? Their team earns money for them.

   A law firm is a good example of this boom trick in action.

   Law firms are essentially legal pyramid schemes. Young lawyers are at the bottom of the pyramid and bill hourly rates that are far less than what a partner could charge for the same work. As such, clients and partners alike often want to have the firm's young associates do a lot of the work because, for clients, it saves them money, and for the partner, it makes them money.

Let's do some math:

Say the firm bills out those young associates to clients at $200 an hour. But what the firm pays them is the equivalent of $100/hour. If we further assume the firm has, say, $50 an hour in overhead for those associates, then each one is making the partnership $50 an hour in profit. Multiplied by 10 associates, that is $500 in profit every hour they work. If they bill five hours a day each, that is $2,500 a day in profit, $12,500 a week, or $50,000 a month. Those 10 associates therefore can generate $600,000 a year in profit to the partnership.

The associates are profit centers, see?

This is the same formula you can use to get rich as a freelancer.

Translated into the world of freelance websites, the way to really rock your freelance career is by becoming an entrepreneur: you can exponentially grow your business and income if you are able to bid on, and get, bigger projects, and preferably, more than one at a time.

Bigger projects mean that you will need to hire subcontractors to whom you can farm out the extra work, just like the law firm that farms out its work to the firm's young associates. Your subcontractors can become *your* new profit center. Do that, and you can multiply your earnings considerably.

So that's the secret. You can bypass the limits of the billable hour by becoming a rainmaker.

Boom!

BOOM YOUR BUSINESS BOTTOM LINE

▶ Just as the advent of online marketplaces have transformed e-commerce, so too have online sites like Upwork and Freelancer transformed the gig economy.

▶ The secret to getting started on sites like these is to (contrary to all other advice in this book) think small. Look for smaller projects to bid on, and also, look at a small niche skill that you can promote. Starting small helps you get the first pickle out of the jar.

▶ Remember, you won't get rich billing by the hour. The key to making big bucks on sites like these is to be entrepreneurial: bid on bigger projects—preferably more than one at a time—and then hire other freelancers to help do the work on the project.

SECRETS OF THE MILLIONAIRE SOLOPRENEUR

If you think you can do it,
or you think you can't do it,
you are right.
—Henry Ford

On that cold, misty, sad, too-early morning, Bucky Fuller stood on the shores of icy Lake Michigan, trying to decide whether or not to kill himself.

His whole life, he had tried to fit in, but it never worked. Bucky had been kicked out of Harvard twice, his beautiful four-year-old daughter had just passed away of complications from spinal meningitis, and his latest venture, The Stockade Company, a small business he ran with his father-in-law, was going under.

Destitute, with nothing but a small life insurance policy left to his name, Bucky thought he might be worth more to his wife and newborn child dead than alive. But in a moment of clarity, he had a realization: "You do not have the right to eliminate yourself. You do not belong to you, you belong to the Universe."

Bucky went home, and the clarity continued. He decided that his essential problem in life had been that he had been taught to listen to everyone else and not to think for himself. He resolved then and there to do just that: to rely on himself and do his own thinking. He reports:

> *I said, "What can a little man [do] in the face of the formidable power of great corporations, great states, and all their know how, guns, monies, armies, tools and information?" Self answering I said, "The individual can take initiative without anyone's permission."*[1]

And so that is what he did. Bucky went on to become a world-renowned architect, author, inventor, entrepreneur, poet, and one of the great, most beloved geniuses of the twentieth century. (For more info, go to BFI.org.)

The individual can take initiative without anyone's permission.

YOU SAY YOU WANT A REVOLUTION

In her great book, *The Million-Dollar, One-Person Business*, Elaine Pofeldt calls the advent of one-person businesses that earn at least seven figures annually a revolution, and she couldn't be more correct. In 2015, she points out, such businesses numbered 35,000 according to the United States Census Bureau, and that was a 33 percent increase from 2011.

By 2017 (the latest year for which such numbers are available), that number had grown to 40,000. Extrapolating, it is easy to see that number easily tops 50,000 now, if not significantly more, especially given the boom in online shopping. This also is not even counting the *several million more* self-employed who earn between $250,000 and $999,000 a year.

According to the Census Bureau:

- There are roughly 30 million businesses in the United States.
- Of those, an incredible 25 million are one-person businesses.

What is exciting about this is that it is entirely feasible to earn a deep six-figure income, and well into the seven figures, even if you are a one-man band (although, as we shall see, any entrepreneur who succeeds this way has a team that he or she relies upon to help make the song sing).

This option takes us well beyond the "freelance fortunes" of the last chapter. While, yes, being able to sell your freelance services on online marketplaces is a great way to earn a nice living and make more money, this plan of action kicks things up a notch.

Think big.

Then think bigger.

Throughout this book you have seen countless examples of people and businesses that have scaled dramatically, often without a lot of help or financial resources. The reason for that, aside from hard work, ingenuity, and pluck, is that it is now easier than ever to start, run, and grow a one-person business.

Tools abound. The internet calls. Technology transcends. Social media provides access. Investors are investing. There is assistance in abundance.

That you can become a solopreneur superstar making big bucks is without question. The tools, insight, strategies, and path are all available for those who know where to look.

Like, for example, in the rest of this chapter.

A HOP, SKIP, AND A JUMP

Long ago and far away, I attended an incredibly powerful three-day entrepreneurship seminar. The event began with the 100 or so participants explaining what their business goals were. Needless to say, most of us shared, in one way or another, how we wanted to grow our businesses.

The seminar leader then engaged us in a very interesting exercise. We all lined up on one side of the room and the leader said, "One by one, I want you to get to the other side of the room, but there's a catch. You cannot cross the room in the same way as anyone who went before you."

We were perplexed, but gave it the old college try.

The first person walked across the room. The next one ran. The next person skipped. By the time it got to me, 30-odd people in, it was getting tough. I hopped across the room. Other people rolled, somersaulted, did cartwheels, and so on.

The point he was trying to make was well taken: even though we all had the same goal, there were at least 100 different ways to get there, and none were "right" and none were "wrong."

Let me suggest that that same lesson applies here. If it is your goal to become a millionaire solopreneur, there are countless ways to get there. But even though they are all different, they are all also essentially the same. It is up to you to find the vehicle that matches your magic, passion, skills, and experience with a product or service that fills a market need, that people want and is something they would be willing to buy.

That product or service has to be something that you can produce or do affordably, and the method for selling it must be simple enough that you can be the hub of a virtual team that can fairly easily execute your vision: what I call the hub-and-spoke system.

Challenging? Yes, a bit. But I bet there are at least 100 ways to get there.

THE PATH OF THE MILLIONAIRE SOLOPRENEUR

Creating a million-dollar solopreneur business is quite different than starting a "regular" business. In the case of the latter, even if the business begins as a solo effort, the plan usually is not to keep it that way, at least not for long. Most businesses intend to grow by adding employees, increasing overhead, moving into nicer digs, getting bigger clients, borrowing and spending capital, and scaling onward and upward.

In the United States, of all small businesses that have at least one employee, roughly five million have 1 to 19 employees, and a tad more than 600,000 have 20 to 499 employees.[2]

Not the millionaire solopreneur business. It is a 100 percent different animal.

A successful one-person, high-growth business is usually designed from the get-go to be just that. Many people who start such businesses are corporate ex-pats who have had their fill of teammates, meetings, bosses, overhead, meetings, feedback, market tests, meetings, and bureaucracy. Wanting a far more streamlined existence, these folks launch their entrepreneurial venture with the specific intent of creating a lean, mean, cash-generating machine.

What sort of businesses are these, and what are some of the different ways to get across this room?

- It could be the real estate broker who specializes in selling apartment houses and works out of a WeWork-type office.
- It might be the e-commerce entrepreneur working from home.
- It is the inventor whose product is manufactured in China and sold in retail stores across the globe.
- It is the drop-shipping master.
- It is the yoga instructor who conquered YouTube.

A yoga millionaire? You bet. Like I said, there are a lot of ways to get from here to there.

Indeed, while it would be difficult to say that anyone "won" the pandemic, if anyone did, it was Adriene Mishler, or as she is better known on YouTube, "Yoga with Adriene." The *New York Times* called her, "The reigning queen of pandemic yoga."

Adriene and her business partner, Chris Sharpe, started posting her friendly, comfortable, free yoga classes on YouTube in

2012. Her following grew slowly until Sharpe began a deep dive into how YouTubers actually searched for yoga classes. It turned out that people did not search for, say, "free yoga," instead they searched for specific classes for specific issues.

Adriene therefore began to create content and classes that fit these most popular yoga-related search terms and keywords: "Yoga for Weight Loss" (her most popular class), "Yoga for Back Pain," "Yoga for Seniors," "Yoga for Skaters," and so on.

Did it work? You tell me. Her top video has more than 30 million views.

By microtargeting her audience with content that resonated within each niche, Yoga with Adriene surpassed 150,000 subscribers by 2015. That started the Adriene snowball. In 2017, her channel surpassed 2 million subscribers.

But it was, of all things, the pandemic that turned Adriene into practically a household name. With everyone stuck and home, stressed out and online, Adriene was in the right place at the right time (or wrong time, take your pick). People discovered her lovely demeanor and gentle way, her spot-on classes, loved that they were free, and flocked to her channel.

Today, Yoga with Adriene has almost 10 million subscribers.

How much does she make a year? We don't exactly know, but certainly it is more than $1,000,000 given that she told the *New York Times* that they "turn down $250,000 to $500,000 a year in ads."[3]

If you need additional ideas, inspiration, tools, or support to help you along your self-employment journey, head on over to my site www.TheSelfEmployed.com where you will find that, and a whole lot more!

Adriene Mishler personifies how many of the strategies discussed throughout this book intersect here, in the one-person juggernaut scenario. Making money while you sleep, building a brand where customers find you, having multiple profit centers, tapping into creative capital—it is all a part of this solo(ish) journey.

Here's the road map.

PICK A PATH, ANY PATH

As with many of the strategies presented in this book, choosing to embark upon the million-dollar solopreneur journey is a deliberate one. This is not something you try to do or hope to do—rather, it is something you intend to do. That means you do not draft a business plan that includes hiring a team (if you draft one at all). Instead, it means you start with a plan that begins and ends with one person—you—being the ringleader.

That analogy is apt because one of the things to understand is that while we are calling this a solo show, it usually is anything but. By that I mean that the most successful solopreneurs create an ecosystem of assistance and assistants that allows them to farm out projects and duties better suited to either specialists or virtual assistants. While you would be the only paid employee of this business, you should plan on hiring several contractors who will help you get the job done.

That said, as Elaine Pofeldt points out, there are essentially five general types of businesses you can start that fit this system:

1. Real estate
2. Professional and personal services
3. Product manufacturing and distribution
4. Information products
5. E-commerce

Several of these will look familiar as they have been discussed elsewhere, but for the purposes of this model, we will share their greatest hits again.

Real Estate

Real estate is an incredible investment, a great business, and a fantastic one-person moneymaking machine. I don't say any of those things lightly. Buying, owning, keeping, and then trading up investment properties is a well-established, tried-and-true way to make a million or more, and in fairly short order to boot.

This is so for several reasons. The main one is called leverage, and it really is the pixie dust of real estate investing.

Let's do a comparison:

Say you want to buy 1,000 shares of Disney stock, which, as of today, is trading at $190 a share. Those 1,000 shares would cost you $190,000.

Ouch.

Now do the same math with a piece of real estate that is selling for $190,000. The beauty of real estate is that you are not required to put 100 percent down to buy that property. Instead, the down payment would likely be 10 percent, or $19,000. The bank would lend you the rest, $171,000.

But who cares? *For $19,000, you would own something worth $190,000.* That's called leverage. You leverage your 10 percent down payment into 100 percent ownership. That means that you get 100 percent of the appreciation of the property and 100 percent of the rents it brings in, not 10 percent.

For $19,000 you would own a property worth almost $200,000. Do you see how incredible that is? For that same $19,000, you would only own 100 shares of Disney. Name me another business or investment where you can put up only 10 percent and own 100 percent.

Beyond leverage, there are four other ways you can make money in a real estate business.

1. **Cash flow.** In real estate, rental income is your cash flow. The more units you have, the greater your cash flow. If you buy the right piece of property, not only will your rental income

pay the property's mortgage, but the extra cash flow is your profit.

2. **Appreciation.** Your equity grows as your property appreciates, in two ways. First, if you look at a graph of real estate prices, it almost always eventually heads upward. That means time alone will increase the value of your property. Second, as the value of your property increases, and as time goes by, you are able to increase your rents, thus creating more cash flow and enabling you to pay down your mortgage faster.

> Your increasing equity can become a self-generating economic growth cycle. When your property increases in value, you can always refinance it, taking some money out. That money can then be used to buy other properties, which will eventually also increase in value, allowing you to pull money out again and buy more property. You can do this again and again, and that is how you get rich.

3. **Tax deductions.** Expenses related to your real estate business are tax deductible. This would include interest paid on your loans, utilities, property insurance, property taxes, upkeep, legal and accounting fees, property management fees, and supplies.

4. **Bigger and better properties.** As you pay down your mortgage, your equity increases. And with increased equity, you can always qualify to get into bigger buildings.

Uncle Sam likes these sorts of upward exchanges because they help the economy and provide for extra taxes. As such, you need to know about something called a 1031 exchange. A 1031 exchange allows you to sell a piece of property, trade up into a bigger property, and not pay taxes (a.k.a capital gains) on the profit until the end of your investment career when you will finally have to pay up.

But by then you will be so wealthy that it will matter a lot less.

Professional and Personal Services

People who offer services for sale and who want to get into the seven-figure club need to figure out how to avoid the tyranny of the billable hour. There are several ways to do that:

Charge more. Chapter 4, "Get Bigger Clients," is critical here. By creating a social following and building a personal brand, you will be able to charge more for whatever it is you do. You can then employ the other part of the law firm model and farm some of that extra work out to contractors.

Your job then, really, is to become a rainmaker.

Get bigger clients. I love small business. You love small business. We all love small business.

And yet.

Small businesses have small business budgets. If you are a professional who provides services—a photographer, a designer, a writer, a lawyer, a computer geek—you are never going to get to the promised land if you continue to concentrate on finding and servicing individuals or small businesses. Needless to say, corporate clients have the budget, track record, institutional wherewithal, and most of all, the desire and intent to pay you what you are really worth.

Sounds nice, right? So how do you get to that side of the room? One way is the way of Dan Pred.

Dan is the owner/proprietor of Video Media in Portland, Oregon (www.VideoMediaPortland.com). A top-notch videographer with top-shelf clients that include HP, Microsoft, P&G Professional, Intel, and the band KISS (to name just a few), Dan does no advertising or marketing at all as all, of his work comes from satisfied former clients and word of mouth.

Dan did the big gig, hire employees, rent an expensive downtown studio thing, but he much prefers his current business model that finds him servicing these world-class clients out of the converted garage behind his house. Aside from a much lower overhead, this allows him the freedom to work when and how he wants, including being able to spend more time with his beautiful young daughter and wife.

Dan has come a long way since the early days when he advertised in the Yellow Pages and shot weddings, bar mitzvahs, and recitals.

How did he get there?

1. **His intention was clear.** Deciding that "corporate clients pay corporate money," he put the word out to his network that he wanted to get into that type of work. A local production company hired him, allowing him to get his foot in the door.

2. **He's great at what he does.** "Corporate clients expect great work, that is a given," and Dan definitely does great work (one client remarked, after seeing him at a shoot for Bank of America in Portland, "I thought they flew him in from New York"). But importantly, Dan points out, "there is also plenty of quality competition." So why does he get repeat business when it might go elsewhere?

3. **He gives great customer service.** "I am very diligent, very service oriented. I return emails and phone calls promptly. I have never missed a deadline. I don't complain. I stay under budget. I get along with everyone, and I am always communicating with the client with regard to the state of the project."

Dan also understands that he can't do everything himself, and that is why he has a team of contractors who help him with overflow—editors, writers, motion graphics specialists, camera operators, and so on.

So this is one way to get across the room: Find big clients who love your work and who are willing to pay big fees. Institute the hub-and-spoke model, hiring help as needed. Keep your overhead low, and do what you love.

Create multiple profit centers. Barbara Winter is the original digital nomad, a workshop leader, entrepreneur extraordinaire, and the author of one of the best business books ever for the solopreneur, *Making a Living Without a Job*. She is also the best proponent of the multiple profit center concept around.

For Barbara, having MPCs is the key to being, as she calls it, "joyfully jobless." Among other things, what is great about this strategy is that you can "audition an idea." You have to be willing to try some new stuff out, to see if it works. You need to discover:

- Do you like it?
- Will other people like it?
- Can it generate enough income?

As a professional, it is almost incumbent upon you to test, try, and perfect additional profit centers if you aim to be a millionaire solopreneur.

Barbara Winter's site, JoyfullyJobless.com, promises:

New ideas, information and inspiration arrive in your mailbox (your real mailbox, not the one on your computer) six times a year when you subscribe to Winning Ways newsletter. Each issue brings you insights on the Joyfully Jobless Journey. You'll find:

- *Profit center ideas and success stories*
- *Book recommendations*

- *Marketing tips*
- *Resources to feed your entrepreneurial spirit*
- *Stories of others who are making a living without a job[4]*

Product Manufacturing and Distribution

Our next option on this path is for the person who wants (or needs) to create his or her own product. This strategy also fits all of our criteria because:

- The income potential for such a venture is significant, but
- The footprint for the entrepreneur can be small.

Of course, you will need to find partners who can manufacture your product, but that's the idea: you are the hub and they are the spokes.

This is what Funlayo Alabi did when she created her business, Shea Radiance (www.SheaRadiance.com). Founded in 2009 in Funlayo's kitchen, Shea Radiance came to be because Funlayo needed "to solve our family's dry skin problems. Both our boys had very dry and eczema-prone skin, and we found shea butter to be the ultimate healing balm."

What Funlayo also discovered was that the best shea butter in the world comes from West Africa. As such, she teamed up with women-owned cooperatives there and sources her shea butter *only and directly* from these women-owned cooperatives. Not only does this provide an economic lifeline for these women, allowing them to be self-sufficient, but it provides Shea Radiance with an affordable source material for her product.

Did the pandemic affect Funlayo's business? Of course, in ways both good and bad. For a while, especially in the beginning, her supply chain was disrupted. But beyond that, on the upside, Funlayo found that our collective newfound passion for washing hands meant that a lot of people, including her female customers, had very chapped hands. "We leaned into that opportunity," she told me. Shea butter products were an obvious solution, and a big hit.

Shea Radiance products are sold online on its website, on Amazon, in health and beauty stores across the country, and in selected Whole Foods markets in the Northeast.

To fund Shea Radiance's growth, Funlayo used various funding sources, including PayPal Working Capital (https://www.paypal.com/workingcapital). With flexible repayment options, no credit check, and funding in minutes, an option like this was especially welcome as Shea Radiance is a women-owned, minority-owned business.

These days, manufacturing a product like Shea Radiance does, while never easy, is easier than in times past. Product manufacturing today can take several forms:

- 3D printing is affordable and quick, given the right product.
- Manufacturers and factories can be found in the United States, in China, indeed almost everywhere across the globe.

Now, you may be asking, "That sounds great, Steve, but how in the heck do I find a factory?" Let me suggest that you check out the site MakersRow.com.

Maker's Row dubs itself, "Your end-to-end manufacturing process—all in one place." It certainly is that. This manufacturing portal gives creators the tools, resources, and contacts necessary to launch a product. You can get consultations, test a product, have small batches made, and find factories. Makers Row boasts "10,000 manufacturers, 100,000 brands, 2 million products made."

The next step is distribution. Selling direct to consumer is one common method, with entrepreneurs setting up websites and selling to the public. Selling on marketplaces like Amazon and eBay is certainly also a possibility. The final frontier would be (to the extent it makes sense) to get the product into retail stores.

This again is where outsourcing and finding the right help becomes necessary.

- Sales reps have contacts you do not have. Getting one to carry and sell your product therefore makes a lot of sense. Another great thing about sales reps is that they work on commission, giving them an incentive to make the sale. Even better—you do not have to pay them until that sale is made.
- Hiring a marketing/SEO/social media expert can help a lot.
- Having a great shipping partner is also key.

You can find sales reps at ZipRecruiter, RepHunter.net, TheOMGrep.com, FindSalesRep.com, and RepResearch.com.

Information Products

It would be difficult to overestimate just how many different ways you can package and sell your knowledge these days: blogs, articles, websites, webinars, workshops, online courses, e-books, e-newsletters, podcasts, and videos are just the tip of the iceberg. If you have specialized knowledge about a specific topic and there is a market for that information, packaging it properly and selling it online is a boom waiting to happen.

That's what Peter Shankman did, although his journey to being a millionaire solopreneur was a bit more serendipitous than most.

Shankman owned a PR company and knew a lot of reporters. He also had a lot of sources and experts for those reporters.
One day, Shankman received a query from a journalist looking for
an expert to interview. He relayed it to his database of sources. It
worked so well that word spread, and soon journalists galore began
to inundate him with requests for experts for stories. Before long,
Peter Shankman had become sort of the go-to guy for reporters
seeking sources.

To better handle the incoming queries, he first created a Facebook group where he could connect the journalists with the sources.
But, as he told me recently, before long, demand overwhelmed supply and even the Facebook group became unmanageable.

Shankman then moved the group over to a custom website
where he was better able to manage the growing email list of
experts and journalists. He dubbed the site and service HARO,
"Help A Reporter Out."

Three times a day, and absolutely free, HARO began to email
queries from journalists and reporters to what was then a list that
had grown to 15,000 folks who hoped to be picked to share their
expertise with the media. Each email contained 50 to 60 media
inquiries.

Needless to say, HARO's open rate was 75 percent.

Shankman created HARO as a passion project but quickly
realized that he had a potential gold mine on his hands. Companies took note of the huge list and open rate of his emails and
asked to advertise there. But "not wanting to spam people," Shankman decided to limit ads to a small text ad of about four lines at
the top of each email that went out to a list that, by the third year,
had swelled to some 500,000 opt-ins.

*That one tiny ad made Shankman, "a million dollars in revenue
in year one,"* a little more than that in year two, and a little more
again in year three. At the end of that third year, one of Shankman's first advertisers, Vocus Inc., offered to buy HARO.

Shankman sold it to the company for $2.5 million.

These days, Peter Shankman is a bestselling author, speaker, podcaster, consultant, and runs a mastermind series called ShankMinds. He also hosts "Faster Than Normal," the number one podcast about living with ADHD (which he calls a "superpower"). You can lean more or work with him at Shankman.com.

When I asked Peter Shankman about HARO's meteoric rise, he was convinced that the service struck a chord quickly because "it was simple—an e-newsletter that didn't change, it helped people, and I gave customers what they wanted."

Wise words.

E-Commerce

We do not need to belabor the potential for e-commerce as a great option for the solopreneur as it has been demonstrated repeatedly throughout this book. Suffice it to say, e-commerce is custom made for the lean, mean, solo machine:

- The cost of entry is low.
- The upside is high.
- Tools to grow continue to proliferate.
- The number of things you can sell is practically limitless.
- Mistakes are not usually very costly.
- Pivots are pretty easy.
- Online is where the eyeballs are.

So, what are you waiting for?

CASE STUDY: DROP-SHIPPING

Drop-shipping is a very unique form of e-commerce and a great example of how a solopreneur can launch a very successful hub-and-spoke business.

As with any e-commerce endeavor, you would need to pick a niche and products, choose an online host for your e-store, build it, create a merchant account to accept payments, and so on. But here's the trick:

Instead of buying and stocking inventory that will sit on your virtual shelves (or in your extra bedroom), *you do not have to buy any inventory at all*. Instead, your site is full of products from a wholesaler or supplier who is the one that actually stores the inventory.

Let me repeat that: you do not have to buy any inventory at all. Consider how much money, time, effort, and overhead that can save you.

Nevertheless, what people see when they come to your e-store is an e-commerce site just like any other: pretty pictures of products and prices, shipping options and so on. For all they know, you have a warehouse full of inventory, except you don't.

Behind the scenes, what customers do not see is that when they buy one of those products, the order goes both to you and the wholesaler, also known in this case as the drop-shipper. The drop-shipper packs and ships the order, and the payment is split between you and the drop-shipper. All customers see is that you stock a product they want, they click and buy it, and then they receive the product a short time later. Given that almost all of the logistics are handled by your drop-shipping partner behind the scenes, being able to run this business as a hub-and-spoke business is quite feasible.

Drop-shipping thus fits both of the requirements that we have been looking for throughout this chapter. Not only does it allow you to run a business as a solopreneur (with help), but it also has the potential to earn you big bucks. Making $1 million yearly is definitely doable, and even if you make less, drop-shipping can still be a very substantive profit center.

If this intrigues you (and it should), here are a few tips for how to get started.

Choose the Right Platform

Shopify is a large, respected, reliable drop-shipping host site. Other good e-commerce host sites that cater to drop-shippers are:

- Amazon
- WooCommerce
- Magento
- BigCommerce
- OpenCart

Find the Right Products

Once you decide upon a platform, you will need a niche and products. Here are the biggest suppliers and wholesalers in the drop-shipping game:

- Spocket
- Salehoo
- Oberlo (used with Shopify)
- BuyerZone
- Dropship.me
- Wholesale Central
- AliDropship
- Alibaba
- Modalyst
- Dropshipping by Dropwow
- Worldwide Brands
- Doba
- DropShip Direct
- Sunrise Wholesale

Note that this list is not exhaustive. If you know of a product that you like and would like to sell, contact the manufacturer and see whether it drop-ships. Many do, even if they do not advertise it.

Start Slow

From their home in Singapore, brothers Steve and Evan Tan launched their first drop-shipping store as a bootstrap operation on Shopify in 2016. The brothers explained to *Business Insider* that making sure the fundamentals are in place is vital to a successful launch.[5]

They list a few areas in particular to initially pay attention to as you launch your first drop-shipping store:

- Make sure the supplier has sufficient inventory.
- Check to see if the warehouse has a record of on-time shipments.
- Create systems in order to be able to handle customer service issues.

Says Steve Tan, "If you grow your business quickly while you're still a team of one or two, it can quickly become unmanageable." The Tan brothers recommend starting slow, with just a few initial products, learning the ropes, hiring help if needed, and automating what you can. "Scaling is the last phase I would recommend," Steve said.

As the Tan brothers told *Business Insider,*[6]

> "Having a team is super important. A lot of people do it alone, but it doesn't have to be that way." Evan said that even really successful dropshipping teams of two-to-three people with 7-figure stores, while lucrative, can be draining. Dropshippers can quickly burn out if they're doing everything themselves, from communicating with suppliers to fielding customer emails. "In order to scale you need a team to support your growth."

Can you do it? Of course you can. Always remember: *"The individual can take initiative without anyone's permission."*

BOOM YOUR BUSINESS BOTTOM LINE

▶ Million-dollar, one-person, solopreneur businesses are on the rise because the internet has made such endeavors far more affordable and doable. Tools, opportunities, assistance, and options abound online for the solopreneur.

▶ Such businesses are never meant to grow into multi-employee endeavors. Rather, they are purposefully begun with the specific plan to keep them solo to the extent possible.

▶ There are five general business types that can fit this mold: real estate, professional and personal services, product manufacturing and distribution, information products, and, of course, e-commerce.

▶ Creating a million-dollar, one-person business typically requires (1) that you create multiple profit centers, and (2) that you bring in the help you need via freelancers to fulfill contracts, handle shipments, and so on.

PART IV

OTHER PEOPLE'S MONEY

We all know it takes money to make money, but it also takes great teammates and creative capital. Check it out.

CHAPTER

IT TAKES MONEY
TO MAKE MONEY

The poor and the middle class work for money.
The rich have money work for them.
—Robert Kiyosaki

Taking your business to the next level almost inevitably requires money. New marketing, drop-shipping, more locations, online expansion, e-commerce, creating a new product line—you name it, money usually solves it.

So, where do you get that money? It typically comes from four sources:

1. **You.** You have assets to use or sell to fund your expansion— stocks, savings, other investments, etc.
2. **Your business.** You can either increase sales, which is the preferable method, or tap into business resources akin to your own assets—leveraging real estate, liquidating assets, and so on.
3. **Investor(s).** Getting outsiders to invest in your business requires having a business that is investable. Axiomatic, yes, but sometimes easier said than done.
4. **Loans.** A loan from family or friends, a bank, or some other entity is of course the tried-and-true way to get the money you need.

That's it. Everything else usually is variations on a theme. Whether it's an SBA loan or a crowdfunding campaign, a micro-loan, a credit card, or a business incubator, the money you seek will inevitably take some form of one of these four options.

Tapping into "other people's money" (OPM) is a valuable trick in your small business boom toolbox. In the next few chapters, a plethora of patronage possibilities are presented.

DEBT AND EQUITY FINANCING

You will notice that of the four options listed above, two require no outside help: using your own assets or those of your business. The other two are the OPM options, loans and investors. Indeed, those two OPM methods are the classic ways entrepreneurs fund business growth.

Another name for them is debt financing and equity financing.

Debt financing is self-explanatory: A business takes on debt via a loan of some sort in order to fund growth. Such a loan might come from a family friend in the early years, or later on, a bank or some other financial institution. To get a significant loan that can propel significant growth, the business must be in a place where (1) money is the solution to growth issues, and (2) that business has the ability to service the necessary loan. Lacking either the specific need, or capability to handle such a loan, debt financing will be out of the question.

Equity financing is different. Equity financing occurs when the business is in a position, and is willing, to exchange an ownership share to an investor in exchange for capital. The television show *Shark Tank* is an example of angel investors. The sharks are angel investors who are willing to give the entrepreneur capital in exchange for an ownership (a.k.a equity) share of the business.

Equity funding in its various forms is discussed in detail in Chapter 16, "Collaboration Nation." Here we will concentrate on bank loans and other forms of debt financing.

PREPARE TO BE INVADED

You have gotten loans before, of course, be it for a car, your home, or your business, and as such, you know the drill: lenders want to know a lot about you, your income, your debts, your payment history, your creditworthiness, and your firstborn before agreeing to lend to you. (OK, maybe I exaggerate, but just a little bit.) You get the point. It may seem that getting that elusive yes from a lender is difficult, but truly it is not. Here is the fact: banks *want* to lend to you.

Banks are in the business of lending money. That is what they do. In fact, banks would prefer that you borrow *a lot of money* because the more you borrow, the more they make. Your job therefore is to make it easy (or at least easier) for them to say yes.

That's the trick and the point.

The good news is that millions of entrepreneurs have figured out how to get a lender to help finance a company's growth. Drive down the street and notice all of the small businesses you see. Look at the buildings they are in and often own. Go online and do a search for all of the businesses in your city, county, state. There are *a lot* of small businesses out there. How many? In the United States, there are almost 30 million small businesses. And if they all found the money, so can you. What one person can do, another can do!

Getting that investment requires two things:

- A business that is ready for funding, and
- Locating the right funding source

Being ready means having your business house in order such that when a lender or investor looks at it, lending you money makes sense. They will *want* to lend to you because your business is so strong, so viable, so ready for growth.

Finding the right source means that you narrow the many options you will see in these next few chapters down to the one or few most likely to give you terms that work best for your business and growth strategy.

PREPARING YOUR BUSINESS FOR A YES

Banks in particular want two things: To lend you money, yes, but also to reduce their risk and exposure to the extent possible. They have a fiduciary obligation to protect their depositors' money by making smart, low-risk loans. So to win this game, you must show them that yours is a low-risk investment.

To determine that, lenders will look at many different criteria:

Your business plan. It may be that you don't have a business plan—many businesses don't. And it may be that you don't want to draft a business plan—most entrepreneurs don't. Too bad. If you want to tap into OPM, whether it is a loan or an investment, you will have to have a business plan.

A business plan is proof that you are not just running your business by the seat of your pants. It is a document that shows how you plan to get from where you are to where you want to be. In it, you analyze your finances, marketing strategy, competition, challenges, opportunities—everything investors need to see in order to properly analyze the strengths (and weaknesses) of your business and its financial situation.

A business plan is also an important document for the business that wants to go boom. Think of it this way: Would a pilot ever fly from Los Angeles to New York without a flight plan? No, of course not. A flight plan tells the pilot which direction to head in, how much fuel will be needed, what the weather conditions are up ahead, landmarks to look for on the way. It is a road map for a successful journey.

Well, that's all a business plan is—it is the entrepreneur's flight plan.

Understanding your business inside and out, knowing your financials cold, and thinking about the opportunities and challenges ahead allows you to be both more strategic and more tactical in your business. Strategically, your plan helps you understand the path for getting to where you want to go. Tactically, it helps you make course corrections as needed since you will know the upside and downside to proposed actions.

- Can you afford to invest in that marketing campaign? Your business plan will tell you.
- Is opening another location a good idea? Your business lends insight.
- Can you afford to pay off that loan early? Review the financials in your plan.

> There are many resources that can help you craft a business plan, but the best one I have found is Liveplan.com. With 500 sample plans, step-by-step guidance, help with financials (without spreadsheets!), and lender-approved formats, you can't go wrong.

The other main thing a lender looks at when determining the strength of the loan applicant and application are known as "the Cs," to wit:

Character. Ideally, you can find a loan that does not require a personal guarantee. Sometimes that is possible, but often not. Again, banks and other lending institutions understandably want to cover their risk, and a loan guarantee by the owner/ CEO/applicant helps do that. As such, your own personal financial character and that of your senior management is in play. You will need to be able to answer questions such as: How is your personal credit? Do you have a history of paying loans back in full and on time? What is your debt-to-income ratio? Have you or your business ever been sued?

Capital. Lenders will want to know the amount of money you are looking to borrow and for what reasons. The loan size and purpose must make sense. In addition, capital refers to the amount of equity the owners have in the business; you must have skin in the game if you want to attract OPM.

Capacity. What is the ability of the business to service the loan? Financial statements help tell this tale.

Collateral. Unsecured business loans are not common. Rather, you and/or the business will likely be asked to collateralize the loan with real estate or other valuable consideration.

Conditions. This factor relates to the economic, regulatory, technological, and other relevant conditions that may affect the ability of the business to service the loan. Is the economy booming, or is it recessionary? What are interest rates like? Is this a heavily regulated industry?

Compliance. Does the business have a record of complying with taxes, legalities (such as the filing of required documents), environmental and safety regulations, and so on?

Finally, and more specifically, financial institutions will also look at various financial ratios when analyzing a business loan application. These include:

Leverage ratio. This ratio consists of your total business liabilities divided by total business equity. Ideally, your assets would be four times your debt (i.e., a ratio of 4 to 1). Of course, the less debt the better.

Loan-to-value (LTV) ratio. When you pledge collateral, the LTV ratio looks at the amount of the loan compared to the appraised value of the collateral. The collateral typically must be of more value than the loan. The idea is that if the loan is defaulted on, the lender will still be able to pay off the loan with the collateral. LTV is calculated by the total dollar amount of the loan divided by the appraised value of the collateral.

Debt service coverage ratio (DSCR). This last ratio sounds more difficult than it really is. The DSCR is your annual net income divided by annual loan payments. This ratio lets the lender understand how many loan payments you could make given your net income. If you are sure to not ask for a loan that will be too difficult for your business to pay, your DSCR will be fine.

> Before applying for a business loan, calculate these ratios. If they are less than ideal, improve them before passing Go if you want to collect more than $200.

The good news is that the bank that is most likely to work with you is the one that knows you and your business best, namely, your present business bank. Do not underestimate how powerful that relationship can be. Think back to your lean startup days. Getting a loan from a bank was likely out of the question because your new business did not have the banking relationships, track record, or the credit history to be loan-worthy. Yet these challenges are likely all gone now. You have a business bank now. You have a relationship with that bank. That is not insignificant. Given that, your present business bank can and should be the first place you look when seeking funding to grow your business.

How to Get a Million-Dollar Loan

Needless to say, to get a million-dollar loan, you need to be able to prove that your business can service a million-dollar loan. The bank will expect:

- **Excellent credit.** Both your business and personal credit ratings need to be superb.

- **At least two years in business.** New businesses are riskier because they have less of a track record to rely upon. The longer you have been in business, the better.
- **$10 million in annual revenue.** To ensure that your business can service such a large loan, the ratios must work, and for the ratios to work, annual income in this range would likely be required.
- **Profit.** Same idea. You need to be able to show that you can repay the debt. A significant profit margin shows that.
- **A personal guarantee.** A personal guarantee or sizable collateral will also be required. Expect the lender to want $1 million in personal equity.

BANK LOANS

Your written loan application has to be spot-on of course, that's a given. But beyond that, aside from all of the Cs and ratios that will be examined and required in your application, you should also expect to have a face-to-face meeting with your banker. Be prepared. Here are the sorts of questions to expect:

Why do you need the money? Not surprisingly, a generalized answer will not cut it. Instead, as with your loan application, you will need to give specific answers. Is the money needed for operations, labor, a new location, asset purchases, a trip to Hawaii, or what?

How much do you need? Asking for too much is a mistake, as is asking for too little. Why do you need *this amount*, and what will you be using it for?

What is a realistic timeline for repayment? The lender will have its requirements of course, but you should also know yours. You will need to explain how the loan fits in to your plans, your revenue projections for this investment, and how all of that fits into the business's ability to repay the loan in a certain time frame.

Is your plan feasible? Your business plan and revenue projections will clarify your strategy for world domination, but be prepared to answer similar questions live.

Are your numbers realistic? Commercial lenders know what they are doing; they have read a few business plans in their time and have seen many, many financial forecasts.

Why you? You have most likely watched ABC's *Shark Tank*. As such, you know that the sharks often say that they invest in the entrepreneur as much, if not more, than the business. So too your lender. Yes, the bank will definitely rely more on cold, hard numbers, but do not discount that, in the end, it is also investing in you.

Bankers know the fluff from the stuff. So you'd better be prepared on two fronts:

1. You must know all of your numbers cold—past, present, and future. How much did you make last year? What was your profit margin? What are your five-year projections if you get the amount requested? What are your customer acquisition costs?
2. Are your forecasted numbers realistic? This is key. These savvy bankers will turn you down straightaway if you offer up pie-in-the-sky projections.

Aside from conventional business bank loans, there are a number of other lending products that may work well to fund your plan:

Business lines of credit. It may be that you already have a line of credit with your bank. Excellent. Why? Because your existing line of credit is the low-hanging funding fruit. Assuming yours is in good standing, getting that credit line increased should be a painless process.

Specialty loans. Your bank also has loans specifically intended to fund business growth—equipment loans and commercial real estate loans, for example.

SBA LOANS

What if I were to tell you that there is an agency of the United States government whose only job is to help you succeed in your business? Wouldn't that be great? And what if I further told you that agency has a yearly budget of over $1 billion and that it facilitates more than 50,000 small business loans a year, totaling more than $15 billion?

Might an agency like that help you get your business funded?

Of course I am speaking of the Small Business Administration, the SBA. I have long said that the SBA is one of the best friends a business can have for all sorts of reasons, but especially when it comes to funding. Yes, the infamous Paycheck Protection Program (PPP) loans that were given out at the start of the pandemic were, let's just be generous and say, "problematic." But that program was fixed, and more generally, most loans that the SBA guarantees run very smoothly.

You might notice that I said that the SBA guarantees loans. It is important to understand that it does not make them. And that is fine by us. By being a guarantor, the SBA makes it easier for lending institutions to say yes because they are assured of repayment; if the borrower is unable to repay, the US government will. Sweet! The amount of the guarantee depends upon the type and purpose of the loan, but generally, it is between 50 percent and 90 percent, although "your results may vary."

One of the truly great things about SBA loans, therefore, is that they are easier to get than conventional loans. Because the SBA guarantees the loan (at least partially), bank underwriting requirements are less stringent. And that means that if your credit, or your business's credit, is less than stellar, you may still qualify for a loan.

> The granddaddy of SBA loans is the 7(a) loan program. 7(a) loans can be used for a variety of purposes—starting up, working capital, inventory, purchasing equipment, even real estate. The length of a 7(a) loan is up to 25 years, depending on the amount, and the maximum loan amount is $5 million (with 75 percent guaranteed by the SBA).

Applying for an SBA loan is essentially the same as applying for a conventional bank loan, although you will need to find a lender that specializes in SBA loans, as not all do. The other difference is that there will be an extra layer of documentation that the SBA requires.

CREDIT CARDS

It is certainly easy to understand why you might want to use your personal credit cards to fund your boom, what with them being so readily available and all. But it is equally true that there are significant downsides to this option. There are definitely pros . . . and cons.

Pros
- **No approval required.** There are no hoops to jump through, no bankers to impress, and you only take on as much debt as you need at any given moment.
- **No need to give up equity.** There will be no shark demanding 40 percent when you swipe your card.
- **Flexible terms.** There will be no 100 percent repayment deadlines, other than self-imposed ones.

Cons

- **Comingling.** Mixing your personal credit with that of your business is not a good idea. One reason you incorporated (you did incorporate, didn't you?) was to separate business and personal assets and liabilities.
- **Liability.** If you are incorporated, and you nevertheless mix personal and business finances, a court may determine that your corporation is nothing but a shell and void the legal and financial protections incorporating affords you.
- **Potentially significant repayment terms.** Running a big balance on your credit cards—be they personal or business cards—means you will repay a lot in interest, especially if your plans go plop.

So, yes, credit cards are great in many ways, but the savvy entrepreneur will have a plan to pay them off as quickly as possible.

FRIENDS AND FAMILY

The "friends and family plan" has funded many a successful venture that has paid off handsomely for both the lenders (the friends and family) and the borrower (the entrepreneur) alike. Example:

- **Albertsons Markets.** Joe Albertson borrowed $7,500 from one of his aunts to help with the $12,500 he need to join the startup partnership. Current sales at Albertsons Markets top $2 billion a year.
- **Pizza Hut.** Dan and Frank Carney borrowed $600 from an insurance payment left by their deceased father to launch the now-ubiquitous pizza chain.
- **Trivial Pursuit.** The two founders scraped together $70,000 from friends, family, and business associates. Each in turn got 1 percent of the company for their investment. Not a bad deal for them, eh?

But, needless to say, there are pros and cons to the friends and family plan too. The pros are that you will likely have very favorable repayment terms. The cons are that if you do not or cannot repay on time, Thanksgiving is going to be very awkward indeed.

And maybe that's why you should look at creative and alternative funding instead. Read on.

BOOM YOUR BUSINESS BOTTOM LINE

▶ Debt financing is a solid option for tapping into OPM. As opposed to equity financing, taking on debt does not require that you take on a partner or investor, and that alone tips the scales for many an entrepreneur.

▶ Your present business bank is where you should look first when looking for a business loan. They know you and want to work with you.

▶ But even if you go to a different lender, the key to getting the money you need is to create a low-risk, high-reward proposal for the lender. Because banks want to say yes to you, your job is to make that an easy decision for them.

▶ Other products and options abound, aside from conventional bank loans. SBA loans, lines of credit, even credit cards make sense in the right circumstances.

UNCONVENTIONAL CAPITAL

Money, pardon the expression, is like manure.
It's not worth a thing unless it's spread around,
encouraging young things to grow.
—Dolly Levi, *Hello, Dolly!*

Sometimes, for whatever reason, tapping into conventional sources of capital is simply not possible. Whether it's credit problems, or an idea that is too unique, or issues of age/ race/gender discrimination, "traditional" funding just isn't in the cards.

Such was the case for Zach Green. Zach enlisted in the Marines at age 18 and soon completed Officer Candidate Training at Quantico. After a successful Marine stint, Zach entered civilian life, but the call of duty soon appeared again in the form of 9/11 and Zach became a volunteer firefighter. It was here that inspiration struck.

I often say that veterans make great entrepreneurs because they can both lead *and* follow, they work well in teams, they can craft and follow through on a plan, are able to pivot on the fly, and are committed to fulfilling the mission. All are strong entrepreneurial traits.

Such was the case with Zach.

Zach quickly realized that keeping track of his helmet and gear in the dark, smoky buildings he was entering was difficult, so he innovated a solution. He began to wrap his helmet and equipment in glow-in-the-dark tape.

A good idea being hard to keep down and all, and with his fellow firefighters encouraging him to run with this great idea, Zach soon turned his clever innovation into a new business. His company, MN8, began to utilize photoluminescent material to create glow-in-the dark firefighting equipment, exit signs, and other safety equipment.

MN8 took off, and we all know what that means: money was needed for payroll, equipment, inventory, and growth. To fund it, Zach dug into the bootstrapper's toolbox, utilizing his savings, credit cards, and home equity to fund his booming business. But it wasn't enough. He had to find additional sources of capital, less well-known sources.

Enter StreetShares. StreetShares is a loan product specifically designed for newer, veteran-owned businesses with low revenue. Zach applied for and got a StreetShares loan, and then, later, a Patriot Express line of credit from the SBA (again, only available to veterans).

It worked.

These days, Zach's company has become a global business, exporting to more than 25 countries, outfitting more than 70,000 firefighters, and Zach Green was named Ohio's Entrepreneur of the Year.

Needless to say, money makes the difference, and so too, the lack of money. The good news is that, especially since the Not-So-Great Recession of 2008, a wide variety of creative funding options have entered the market. You are no longer forced to try to fit your round money peg into a square funding hole—no, these days you can almost always find the right money for the right price if you look closely.

So let's do that.

ALTERNATIVE LENDING

"Alternative lending" is a catchphrase for a variety of private loan products that are not associated with banks and other traditional lenders. Some of these options are unique loans from nontraditional sources, others are altogether different. Either way, one of the best things about these options is that if a less-than-stellar credit history is your issue, funding can still be yours because your credit score is usually less of a deciding factor.

These alternatives tend to be easy to apply for, and decisions and funding are quick, sometimes within 24 hours. Repayment terms are quick too, however, with some requiring full repayment in under two years (as opposed to five years and much longer for traditional lenders). And too, loan amounts are smaller and alternative lender fees tend to be significantly higher. But as a quick, easy source of ready capital, they can't be beat.

Merchant Cash Advances

A merchant cash advance (MCA) is akin to an advance on a paycheck, except in this case, the borrower is a business and the repayment comes not from a job and paycheck, but from future credit card sales. Obviously, such funds are available only to businesses that have a steady stream of credit card sales as repayment is automatically deducted from those sales.

It works this way: A small business in need of financing can find an MCA company and apply for a loan. Because the small business's future credit card sales secure the debt, the MCA company can make almost immediate lump-sum funding available. The advance can be a few thousand dollars up to $100,000 or more.

MCA loans are not inexpensive. You will pay a "factor rate" between of 1.2 percent and 1.4 percent. So, for example, say that you want to borrow $10,000 and the factor rate is 1.3 percent. You would need to pay back $13,000, in about 18 months or so.

Factoring

A similar option is called factoring, except that here, instead of relying on future credit card sales, the company lending the capital (called a "factor") will look at your accounts receivables.

Let's say that you have a client who owes you $10,000 for services rendered, and the client has a policy of paying net 90, but you need that money right now. A factor would buy that asset (the money owed to you) from you, giving you less than it is worth, and the factor would then get paid by your client.

You can quickly see the downside to this option—your client knows that you sold its obligation to you. A tad uncomfortable to say the least, but hey, quick money is quick money.

The next two options are unique in that they have absolutely nothing to do with any sort of lending company. Instead, they are options that come from business associates.

Supplier Financing

In his great book *Starting on a Shoestring*, author Arnold Goldstein explains how, back in the day, he launched a business called Discount City with $120,000 of merchandise, $20,000 worth of fixtures and shelves, and three months of deferred rent. Out of his own pocket?

$2,600.

How did Goldstein pull off this magic trick? Supplier financing. Goldstein explains that, in the right circumstances, a supplier, vendor, or wholesaler just might help fund a business with:

- Products (on consignment)
- Products bought on credit (with deferred repayment terms)
- Deferred rent (with interest)
- Actual money in the way of loans (with very high interest rates)

Why would a supplier do this? To create a new customer. If you can structure the deal such that the vendor's exposure is limited (by, for instance, having all products owned by the vendor and sold by you on consignment), and you can prove that you will become (or remain) a viable, valuable customer, it just might behoove the vendor to help you out because it would be in its self-interest to do so.

Clearly, such deals are not well publicized and not easy to get for obvious reasons. That said, they do happen, and so, if you have a strong relationship with a major supplier, it just may be that it would be more interested in working with you than you may realize.

> I'm convinced that about half of what separates
> the successful entrepreneurs from the non-
> successful ones is pure perseverance.
> **—Steve Jobs**

Seller Financing

This last little gem only works if you are looking to buy an existing business. In this scenario, you would need to find a business that you want to buy *and* a seller that would be willing to finance all or part of the purchase.

In this sense, it is like a home buyer looking to buy a home where, in the lingo of real estate, the seller is willing to "carry the papers," that is, the seller acts as the bank and the buyer pays the seller directly, instead of getting a loan and mortgage. Home sellers do this sort of thing in down markets where finding buyers is difficult.

Typically, an owner would consider financing the sale of his or her business because:

1. It's a slow market and/or a bad economy. Seller financing helps make a sale more possible.

2. The seller is highly motivated to sell—maybe he is getting divorced, or she is having health issues.
3. It is a bad business. The business is a lemon and the owner thinks that agreeing to finance it will make a deal more likely.

Your job is to figure out which reason it is—numbers 1 and 2 are fine, but avoid number 3 at all costs.

UNIQUE LOAN OPTIONS

There are many funding choices that do not fall under the penumbra of "traditional lending" but which, nevertheless, are either made by, or associated with, banks and other lending institutions.

Microfinance /CDFIs

Microloans are for microbusinesses. They tend to be small—anywhere from $500 to $25,000 is typical. But as such, even if you have poor credit, getting a microloan is still possible because the small size of the loan makes it a smaller risk. In fact, your FICO score may be less important to a microfinance lender than your passion, experience, and the opportunity.

Several sources are available to you for microfinancing:

Community Development Financial Institutions (CDFIs). CDFIs make very affordable microloans to historically underrepresented communities and organizations in order to foster minority entrepreneurship. A Google search for CDFI and your location will give you many options.

The biggest funder of CDFIs in the United States is Bank of America, which makes more than a billion dollars of loans available yearly to more than 250 CDFIs nationwide.

Accion. Accion.org is a pioneer of microlending in America. It offers loans from $500 on up. The average microloan size in its Chicago office, for example, is $9,000.

Grameen America. Grameen Bank invented microlending in Bangladesh when it started to give out unsecured $100 loans to the local peasants (who had a repayment rate of 97 percent!) Grameen America's maximum first-time loan is $1,500.

Kiva.org. Kiva is also an international organization. It came to the United States in 2010. Loans amounts in the United States are higher, up to $10,000, and interestingly, all loans are funded by user donations.

The SBA. The SBA is a major guarantor of microloans for third-party lenders. The average SBA microloan is $13,000.

In 2005, Chancey Peake began to make what would become her soon-to-be-loved, almost-world-famous banana bread. After losing her day job, Chancey and her husband decided to sell her bread at their local farmer's market. The bread was a hit from the start, and the legend of Chancey Peake's "Banana Manna" began to grow.

Unfortunately, her business was stunted because the farmer's market was only a one-day-a-week deal. Chancey needed a store, but without a job and only a part-time business, getting a loan was next to impossible. Except it wasn't.

Chancey applied for and got a $2,000 microfinance loan from Kiva.org and, even with that little amount of startup capital, was able to rent and launch her own bakery. She now sells 15 varieties of banana bread and has employees thanks to microfinance.

Funding for Minorities

In this era of #BlackLivesMatter, the issue of inequality in all its ugly forms is rightfully before us. While solutions vary, to me, one of the best things that we as a society can do to equalize the playing field is to increase funding and education for disadvantaged would-be entrepreneurs generally, and for African American entrepreneurs specifically.

We entrepreneurs know that building a business changes lives and creates ripples. Small business ownership fosters wealth and jobs, nurtures pride, enhances and stabilizes communities, creates a tax base, helps to fund better schools, and overall, generates hope and optimism.

So, yes, one answer to racial inequality is money; specifically, increased funding for grants and loans to minority small business owners. It is much needed.

> According to the Aspen Institute, *"Hispanic and black Americans have levels of net worth that are only one-tenth of those held by white Americans, and fewer of their assets are in the form of business assets."* And yet, "Families in which the head of the household was self-employed had a median net worth five times that of households in which the head worked for someone else." The report went on to note that "[B]lack entrepreneurs have levels of wealth mobility equal to those of white entrepreneurs."[1]

Given this, it is heartening to see the recent increase in funding for minority entrepreneurship.

Minority Business Development Agency (MBDA). Part of the Department of Commerce, the MBDA is an agency that provides a variety of financing options—loans, grants, and so on. It also has MBDA centers across the country, providing financial advice and mentorship for minority business owners.

SBA programs. The Community Advantage Loan Program offers loans up to $250,000 for businesses in historically underserved communities. The 8(a) Business Development Program offers workshops, training, and, potentially, government contracts to minority-owned businesses.

Private loans. Balboa Capital Corporation offers a Minority Small Business Loan of up to $250,000, *unsecured*. The Business Consortium Fund is a CDFI nonprofit that funds minority-owned businesses through the national Minority Supplier Development Council.

Accion. With offices in 50 states, Accion offers loans from $500 up to $300,000.

Funding for Veterans

Especially since the Iraq and Afghanistan wars, funding for veteran entrepreneurs has also increased. Today, almost one out of every 10 businesses in the United States is owned by a veteran.

Money is available.

The Veterans Administration (VA). The VA has a great small business resource center, the Veteran Entrepreneur Portal. It also offers grants to service-disabled veterans via the Vocational Rehabilitation and Employment program (VR&E).

SBA Veteran Programs. Not surprisingly, our friend the SBA also has a lot of resources for veterans, including, specifically, the Office of Veterans Business Development (OVBD), which provides training and access to capital.

"Bunker in a Box" is a program designed to be a first stop for veterans exploring entrepreneurship. By using videos, online tutorials, and content, veterans can embark on 14 different "missions" that teach entrepreneurship. A similar program, run by the SBA, is called "Boots to Business."

Funding for Women

Women-owned businesses doubled in the 20 years between 1997 and 2017, and now constitute 40 percent of all businesses in the United States. There are a lot of funding and resource options available to them.

The SBA. Start your search with the SBA Office Women Business Ownership Page.

The US Women's Chamber of Commerce. Offers access to "quick, easy, affordable" loans through its partner, Lending Club.

Grameen America. Microloans are available for women-owned businesses for women living below the poverty line.

Angel investors. Funding from angels specifically for women-owned business is available through Golden Seeds and Pipeline Angels.

National Association of Women Business Owners (NAWBO). NAWBO has chapters throughout the country offering training, networking, and access to capital.

Funding for the LGBTQ Community

It is not surprising that members of the LGBTQ community lean toward entrepreneurship given that discrimination against them in the workplace is still very real. As such, funding options for this community is also very real.

Opportunity Fund. This CDFI specializes in serving the underrepresented, including LGBTQ entrepreneurs.

Backstage Capital. This is an early-stage fund that invests in entrepreneurs who are women, people of color, and LGBTQ.

Gaingels. This program connects LGBTQ entrepreneurs with angel investors, mentors, resources, and access to capital.

CROWDFUNDING: IT'S NOT A LOAN, IT'S NOT AN INVESTMENT, SO WHAT IS IT?

As mentioned, for hundreds of years, maybe thousands, there were two and only two ways to borrow money. Either you could take out a loan (from a bank, Uncle Max, or whomever), incur debt, and owe the money, or you could find an investor and sell part of your business, not have to pay the loan back, but instead share your business equity and profits with a new partner.

That's it, two options—debt financing or equity financing.

There are pros and cons to each, of course. Loans allow you to remain the sole owner, but taking on debt is never fun. Selling equity is nice in that you do not have to pay the money back, but having a partner means you are not the only sheriff in town anymore.

That is why, among other reasons, the advent of crowdfunding was such a revolutionary concept. With crowdfunding, you get people (the "crowd") to invest small amounts of money into your business, but it's not a loan because you do not have to pay it back. It is also not a sale of equity, because they do not become your partners. So, what is it?

It's something new, that's what. It's called rewards-based crowdfunding.

In exchange for their investment, you the entrepreneur agree to give the investors a reward of some sort, related to your business or product. For example, say you want to open a food cart. In exchange for an investment of $100, you might agree to name one of your dishes after the investor for a month. Or maybe you own a maple tree farm and have invented a better maple syrup. You could agree to give investors a discount on your syrup.

See? Crowdfunding is not a loan, and it is not an equity investment. It is a "rewards-based investment," and in that there really is something new under the sun. Rewards-based crowdfunding serves two functions. First, it is, obviously a way to fund an idea, project, or business. But also, and maybe equally importantly, crowdfunding is an excellent way to inexpensively test-market a product. If you use your new and improved maple syrup as the reward, you can quickly discover if there actually is a market for it.

How Crowdfunding Works

Crowdfunding is a multistep process.

First, you need something to sell. Crowdfunding works best for things like a product or a specific project.

Next, you need to choose the right site. Kickstarter of course is the big name in the crowdfunding game, but there are many others, and often they are specific to a particular industry (but not necessarily). Here are some other options:

- Indiegogo: similar to Kickstarter
- GoFundMe: fundraising for a cause or individual
- ArtistShare: a crowdfunding site for creatives
- inKind: a site for restaurants
- IFundWomen: help for female entrepreneurs

Once you have chosen the right site, you need to post your project or product. Tell your story. Who are you, what is your dream, why is this a great idea, and why would an investor choose to back it? You will need some marketing materials to tell this story, including a great product description, pictures, and a compelling video.

Next, you need to think through your funding goal. How much do you need, and why? Kickstarter uses an all-or-nothing model in which you need to raise 100 percent of your goal to receive the pledged funds, so don't ask for too much.

You also need to carefully consider your rewards. Rewards are tiered—the more people give, the more they get. So you need to also consider your rewards and figure out what you can reasonably give people in exchange for their hard-earned dollars. As Kickstarter says, "Why do people back projects? To start, they want to support what you're doing. But they also want to feel like they're getting something in return—and rewards let them share in your work."

Don't be like the Coolest Cooler. Coolest Cooler is one of the best-known, most highly funded, and most disastrous Kickstarter campaigns of all time. The high-tech cooler *was* a cool idea—it incorporated a blender, phone chargers, a Bluetooth speaker, LED lights, and things like plates, knives, and bottle openers.

The campaign went viral and raised over $13 million dollars back in 2014.

Unfortunately, a series of mishaps marred the rollout of the product, most notably several problems with production, and President Trump's trade war with China (where the cooler was being manufactured), resulting in a huge jump in tariffs that the company had not nearly budgeted for.

In the end, a third of the backers never received the reward they were promised (the cooler), Coolest Cooler was sued by the State of Oregon and agreed to repay those backers with $20 each, and finally, the company went out of business in 2019.

The next step is promotion. Creating a crowdfunding program is a marketing effort extraordinaire. Do not make the mistake that too many crowdfunders make, thinking that all they need to do is throw their great idea up on the site and they will somehow get $10,000 or whatever.

No, instead, the key to a successful crowdfunding campaign is treating it like the major marketing program it is. You need a great video of course, but you also need to market the heck out of your page. Tell people you know, send it out to your list, have your dad tell his friends, tell the press, build buzz, let the world know what you are doing.

There are two last steps. First, be sure to communicate. Give people regular updates about your progress. Finally, once you hit your goal and get funded, fulfill your rewards, pronto.

CREATIVE ENCOURAGEMENT

Finally, these last two creative funding options are not easily categorized, but they are good to know about nonetheless.

Business Plan Competitions

The New Venture Championship (NVC), presented by the University of Oregon's Lundquist College of Business and now in its thirtieth year, "is a six-round business competition that inspires young entrepreneurs to develop their business dreams into a reality. Teams of graduate and undergraduate students from around the world join the event every year to pitch their business plans and compete for $50,000 in total cash awards."

Business plan competitions happen across the country and are a very interesting way to raise a round of funding for your business venture. They are, as the name implies, competitions where businesses share their business plans through various rounds in front of a panel of judges. In the end, the team/business deemed to have the best plan wins cash and prizes (such as computers, printers, legal assistance, and so on).

For example, Alison Alvarez and Tomer Borenstein founded their tech company BlastPoint in 2016. The computer scientists started a business that sought to leverage artificial intelligence (AI) for large entities like banks and public utilities. The problem was, they had very little startup capital; even the friends and family route was not a viable option.

So they decided to try to bootstrap their business by entering business plan competitions, and it worked. According to an article on Inc.com, "In the past four years, the company has won four such competitions, ranging in size from 2017's UpPrize, which came with a $160,000 reward, all the way to a small $2,000 payoff in the GSV Labs AI Pitch competition in 2020."

Alvarez has four tips for winning such competitions:

1. **Know the judging criteria for each competition.** Judges are given guidelines as to what weight to give different criteria. Ask for those.
2. **Tell real stories.** Stories engage people. A story of how your business did or could help in a real situation makes your pitch more memorable.
3. **Have a hook.** Judges see *a lot* of pitches over the course of a competition. Give them a reason to remember yours.
4. **Have your elevator pitch down.** Alvarez boiled her AI data analysis down to, "It's big data for human brains."

Business Incubators and Accelerators

Financial assistance does not always have to be about money (although money sure is nice). In the business world, it can also take the form of in-kind contributions—things like free or reduced rent, coaching and pro bono legal help, and so on. That's where business incubators and accelerators come in.

A business incubator or accelerator is an entity that houses businesses and provides them with help—computers, support staff, office space, help with payroll, and, importantly, mentoring and access to funding via the network of people associated with the incubator.

Typically, these entities are for new businesses that are past the very early startup phase. Getting into one is not easy, but if you are able to do so, you will find a great network of people ready to help you boom. Of course, that is what the incubator itself is designed to do, but also, angel investors know that they can often find great businesses at these organizations, so they too are in the orbit.

The main difference between an accelerator and an incubator is that the former is a nonprofit, often associated with universities. The latter are for-profit and, as such, will usually require a share of your equity to get in. And because of that, larger financial fish tend to swim there.

Either way, your chances of success, and finding the money you need, are increased by associating with an incubator or accelerator, or, as we are about to see, with some other collaborator.

> If you are looking for unconventional funding—or even conventional funding—then I suggest you check out the book *Target Funding* by Kedma Ough. It is a terrific resource that helps you locate needed funds based on type, industry, demographics, and much more.

BOOM YOUR BUSINESS BOTTOM LINE

▶ It is not only an incredible time to be in business altogether due to all of the programs and assistance that are available today, but in particular, it is a great time to plan a business boom because there are more creative funding mechanisms for small business than ever before.

▶ The savvy entrepreneur will look at this universe of options—everything from factoring to supplier financing to business incubators and accelerators—and tap into the one that can most likely fund that boom—because there definitely is at least one.

▶ Minorities in particular have a lot more funding options these days.

▶ Do not make the mistake of thinking that crowdfunding is simply free money. It is anything but. To succeed in that world takes planning, hard work, creativity, and perseverance.

CHAPTER

COLLABORATION NATION

Alone we can do so little. Together we can do so much.
—Helen Keller

"We were the two slowest, fattest kids in the class."
Ben Cohen was talking about how he met Jerry Greenfield, the man who would eventually become his small business partner, then his big business partner, and always his best friend.

Ben & Jerry did many things right along their long and winding road to ice cream superstardom, but for starters, they laid a vital foundational brick in that road when they heeded Helen Keller's advice and teamed up. When you are on a boom quest, working together almost always beats working alone. And that was certainly true for Ben & Jerry; they admit that the things they were able to accomplish together were so much more than what they ever could have accomplished alone.

To wit: After years of hanging out in high school, the pals went off to different colleges. Afterward, they met up again and started rooming together in New York. As Ben told the *Independent* newspaper, "All our friends had real jobs. Jerry wanted to be a doctor but was rejected by all the medical schools he applied to. I wanted to be a potter, but, after going to a lot of craft shows and trying to sell my pottery, I realized that nobody was ever going to buy it."[1]

Their bad fortune was our good luck. Says Jerry, "Since we'd always liked to eat, we thought we'd do something with food."

They first considered opening a restaurant, but that proved cost-prohibitive. Next they looked at bagels or ice cream since those seemed simpler, cheaper. "One day we went into a place selling used restaurant equipment, and we worked out that it would cost $40,000 to get into the bagel business. We figured ice cream had to be cheaper, so we took a $5 correspondence course in ice cream technology and started making ice cream in our kitchen."

In 1978, they bought a dilapidated gas station in Vermont, fixed it up, and opened their first ice cream shop. Through trial, error, good luck, and savvy, the business ultimately took off, after Ben came up with the idea of packaging their ice cream in little pints and selling it in stores. A whole new category of food was born.

The moral of the story is that it took the combined talents of both Ben and Jerry to create Ben & Jerry's. Says Jerry, "Ben is the creative driving-force of the company, and I am in the supportive role. A classic entrepreneur, Ben is a real risk-taker. And he is never satisfied, which is great for the business. I am pretty cautious, and without Ben as a partner I would never have started the ice-cream business."

Additionally, had it not been for Ben, they never would have invented the trademark chunks that make their concoctions so tasty and unique. Ben suffers from anosmia, a lack of the sense of smell, which also affects taste. As such, from the start, he insisted that their creamy, decadent ice cream include chunks of chocolate, cherries, whatever, as it allowed him to rely on "mouth feel," which he had come to rely on as a substitute for taste buds.

Ben and Jerry are proof that getting the help and money you need can look different ways. In some cases, it means finding the perfect partner—a Jerry to your Ben. At other times, assistance might look like funding from investors, the launch of a joint venture, or finding the right mentor.

> Ben & Jerry fun fact: None of their original flavors are still around. "Just look at this list of our original pint flavors: Oreo Mint, French Vanilla, Chocolate Fudge, Wild Blueberry, Mocha Walnut, Honey Coffee and Honey Orange. You won't find any of them in your grocer's freezer aisle."[2]

However it looks, it is a fact that scaling a business most often comes not from being and acting alone, but rather, from the shared passion, joint commitment, combined resources, and common vision that result from drafting the right team.

When that happens, the whole definitely becomes greater than the sum of the parts.

PARTNERS AND JOINT VENTURERS

Ben needed Jerry. Johnson needed Johnson. Jobs needed Wozniak. Procter needed Gamble. Hewlett needed Packard.

Whom do you need?

As you know only too well, and as has been demonstrated throughout this book, the bravado, competence, and vision that are the entrepreneur's trademark are also the very things that can be our Achilles' heel. The singular vision that allows an entrepreneur to create an entire business out of whole cloth can look like stubborn narcissism when turned inside out. The ability to juggle many eggs at once can result in a lot of broken yolks if the time to share the load is ignored.

That's where finding a business partner comes in. The yin to your yang can create a powerful gang.

Partners

Generally, there are two reasons why people look for business partners: Either they want someone to share the load, or they don't have money and need help.

In the first scenario, it makes a lot of sense to partner with someone since it makes things easier in so many ways. A partner gives you another pair of hands—literally and figuratively. He or she should also prove to be a good sounding board, allowing the two of you to share and bounce ideas off one another. Partners can also lighten the load by sharing responsibilities.

> On the occasion of Bernie Taupin's seventieth birthday, and the fiftieth year of working and writing together, Elton John wrote this to his longtime partner: "Dear Bernie, without you, I would never have had the life I have had. What an eternal gift God gave us. I love you more than ever my angel. Happy Birthday to my dearest friend and collaborator."[3]

Not insignificantly, indeed maybe most significantly, a good partner should fill your gaps. As you know, you have certain skills and abilities, but, like anyone, you lack others. The perfect partner will fill many of those voids. If you are good at marketing, you might need a partner whose skill set is finances. You bring what he or she lacks and vice versa. Ben is the visionary entrepreneur, Jerry is his pragmatic counterweight.

What should you look for in a partner? There are several qualities that make a difference. For starters, you want someone whom you can trust, whose judgment you respect, and whose values are like yours. You need a person whose skills complement your own and who has experience, resources, resourcefulness, integrity, and a strong work ethic. Finally, and not insignificantly, consider camaraderie carefully. You need a partner you would like to spend 10-hour days with.

> **Paulie:** "I don't get it, what's the attraction?"
>
> **Rocky:** "I don't know, she fills gaps I guess"
>
> **Paulie:** "What's gaps?"
>
> **Rocky:** "She's got gaps, I got gaps, together we fill gaps."
>
> *Rocky* (1976)

While the upsides of finding the right partner are significant, the relationship does not come without real risks.

The major risks are legal and financial. Let me put my attorney's hat on for a moment. A business partnership is a lot like a marriage in several ways: the need for a shared vision, a division of labor, joint responsibility, and so on. The most important similarity, though, is that, like a spouse, *either partner alone can take on debt and legal obligations that the entire partnership is liable for.*

I once represented a partnership of four people. One day, the marketing partner decided to sign a contract for an ad in an expensive magazine. None of the other partners had ever agreed to this expense or contract, yet the entire partnership became liable for this $40,000 debt. So legal snafus are a real risk and something of which to be wary.

With that caveat in mind, and despite the risks, for many people, partnerships have proven to be an excellent way to form or grow a business.

> It is vital that you reduce your arrangement with your partner to a written partnership agreement. Writing it down is vital for all sorts of reasons. First, people remember things differently.

Second, people lie. Third, people die. A written agreement will preclude any of those calamities from sinking the ship.

Your partnership agreement should cover all aspects of your arrangement and all contingencies. It needs to spell out who will do what, who invested how much money, how profits are to be distributed, what will happen should one of the partners pass away, agreed-upon ways to end the partnership, and distribution of assets upon dissolution.

Because of its importance, your partnership agreement should be drafted by a lawyer. You don't perform surgery on yourself, and you should not represent yourself in such vital legal matters. Get a partnership agreement and get it done right.

The other reason that people seek partners is that some partners bring money to the table.

Partners with Money

Monied partners can be great because, well, you know why. Yet it is that very money that might make your job doubly difficult. As we all know, money is power. As such, when you bring in a partner because she has the money you lack, your relationship could begin on inherently unequal footing. In that case, you need to level the playing field. You do so by making sure that your potential partner values your sweat equity as much as you value her real equity.

It might help to think of it this way: Let's say that you and your partner want to buy a fixer-upper duplex and your partner has the $50,000 needed to get a loan and buy the place. Further, let's say that you are the one who will be doing all of the fixing up. In that case, this type of relationship can become an equal partnership, but *only if* your sweat equity is valued (legally and emotionally) as much as her capital.

Your job then is to find a partner with money who will respect you and your skills as much as you respect her and her cash.

(Note: There are two kinds of partners with money. One is that person who wants to be part of the day-to-day operations of the business. That is the type we are discussing here. The other is a partner who wants to be a passive investor, essentially an angel investor. That sort of partner is examined later in this chapter.)

Where do you find a partner with money? There are a few places:

The usual suspects. The first and best place to find a potential partner is in your own network of friends and colleagues. Especially in this post-pandemic era, when work was turned topsy-turvy upside down, people more than ever want to do something that means something. You may find that there are a lot more folks in your universe willing to take a risk with you if it means being able to potentially reach escape velocity from the grind.

> *An entrepreneur is a person willing to take*
> *a risk with money to make money.*
> **—Marty Strauss** (my long-gone sweet dad and still
> the best entrepreneur I ever knew)

Friends can be also great business matchmakers, as can lawyers, accountants, bankers, real estate agents, and members of your congregation.

Put the word out.

Work colleagues. My dad met the man who would become his business partner when they were just starting their careers, working as furniture salesmen. Dad had the sales and advertising chops, Phil had the startup capital.

That you have coworkers who may be as disgruntled and inspired as you is probably not unlikely. By the same token, speak with other work colleagues, sales reps, and if you have a business already, possibly even employees and customers (though caution is advised there). Because these people know you and your business, they may be a great resource for matching you with people they know who might be interested in the sort of opportunity you can offer.

The last place to look is online. LinkedIn especially, being the B2B marketplace that it is, can be an excellent source for finding a potential partner with capital to invest.

If you are fortunate enough to find a potential partner, make sure to do your due diligence. Don't fall under the ether and get so intoxicated by someone's money that you fail to vet them thoroughly. Check their background, work history, litigation history, social profiles, and credit.

Joint Ventures

As mentioned, finding the right teammates can take many forms. Oh sure, locating an investor or a partner with money is great, but it's the low-hanging fruit on the assistance tree, even if it is not always ripe or so easy to pick.

Locating a person or company to team up with for a joint venture requires a little more ingenuity, but it is easier in the sense that it is "cleaner." Both parties enter into the relationship on equal footing, mutual goals are agreed upon, and the project is typically for a finite period of time. If I may go back to a previous analogy, while a partnership is like getting married, a joint venture is akin to dating.

There is a lot to be said for the joint venture as a growth tool. For starters, you share the costs and the risks. It also allows your business to enter new markets, on a test basis, and by so doing, you can generate revenue quickly and cost-effectively. Moreover, your business will get introduced to potential new clients. And finally, and importantly, joint ventures build your brand.

A joint venture can be for almost any project or task. Maybe you have invented a better mousetrap but have no way to distribute it. A joint venture with a retail outlet might work. Or maybe you want to launch a big event. You could partner with a venue, or a marketing company, or a band. Look for companies out there with whom you are simpatico and put out some feelers.

Once you have some meaningful leads, one key to success is to clearly define the goals of the venture. Nolo.com (my favorite do-it-yourself legal site) suggests that you:

> *Spend time focusing on whether your two companies are a good fit. [Get] to know the people you'll be working with and the core values of the business. What is their attitude toward collaboration? Do the business leaders share your level of commitment? Will the corporate cultures of your two companies mesh?*

Boston Consulting Group (BCG) is one of the largest, most respected business consultancies on the planet. Not long ago, BCG surveyed 70 executives in 10 different industries to see how to best make joint ventures work. BCG came away with several key takeaways:

1. **Have clear objectives.** Make sure up front to discuss objectives, expected contributions, and concerns.
2. **Put the agreement in writing.**
3. **Tap customers**, suppliers, distributors, employees, and other resources to help support the venture.
4. **Consider "unconventional alliances."** Consider possibly partnering with competitors or even customers.
5. **Utilize and rely on each company's core competencies.**
6. **Dedicate a team to the venture.** BCG found that 83 percent of high performers dedicated a team to the venture, both before and during its execution.
7. **Plot your exit in advance.** The companies that made joint ventures work the best had a clear idea of the beginning, middle, and end of the venture, right from the start.[4]

When Bad Things Happen to Good Ventures

Tiffany & Co. once teamed up with Swatch Watch on a 20-year joint venture project to have Swatch sell its watches under a new brand dubbed the Tiffany Watch Co. The two companies were to share the profits, but after four years of having Tiffany drag its heels on the project, Swatch sued. An arbitration court in the Netherlands dissolved the partnership and ordered Tiffany to pay Swatch $448 million.[5]

ANGEL INVESTORS

When it comes to getting money from an investor, let me suggest that there is no better education you can have than the words and insights of the sharks on ABC's *Shark Tank*. The show demonstrably displays how investors think, what they look for, what weight they give to different investment factors (company financials, market opportunity, etc.) and much more. The show:

- Lets you see how investors analyze businesses
- Helps you understand how much thought and work go into creating an investable business or product
- Shows you what happens when entrepreneurs drink their own Kool-Aid and sink too much time and money into ideas that *they alone* think are great

I have had the pleasure of interviewing several of the sharks over the years—for my column, for my podcast, and for this book. Their insights can help you land an angel investor because that's what a shark is—an angel investor under a different name.

Barbara Corcoran really has a great rags-to-riches story. The daughter of a working-class family of 10 children, she is dyslexic, flunked several courses in high school, and graduated with a D average. After finally graduating college, she had 20 jobs by the time she was 23. She started her company, the Corcoran-Simone Group, with her boyfriend, who loaned her the $1,000 she needed to launch it, but she ended that partnership seven years later when he said he was going to marry her secretary.

After she formed The Corcoran Group thereafter in the late seventies, things started to take off. She became a high-profile real estate agent in New York and eventually sold her company in 2001 for $66 million.

Barbara told me that the key thing she looks for when making an investment is not the financials (though they are important) and not the market opportunity (also important), but rather, it's the entrepreneur him- or herself: How passionate are they? How do they handle rejection? Do they bounce back? Are they resilient? These things, to Barbara, are the most important investment considerations.

Lori Greiner is of a different mindset. She told me that while the cut of the entrepreneur's jib is certainly important, more vital is the product's sales history: that is, for her, the most important thing when making an investment is the product. "To me, the product is number one. I like products that fill a need and hit a broad audience. I always say I can tell if a product is a hero or a zero."

And what about Mr. Wonderful himself, Kevin O'Leary? If you have ever watched the show, you know that O'Leary's main consideration is the numbers. Do they make sense, do they add up?

There is one last "shark" I want to share with you. His name is Baybars Altuntas, an incredibly successful entrepreneur in Turkey and one of the original "dragons" in the Turkish version of the show, *Dragons' Den*.

Baybars and I worked closely together in an organization called the World Entrepreneurship Forum, as well as being coauthors of a book, *Planet Entrepreneur*. His take regarding what dragons/sharks/investors look for is the best I have ever heard. Here's his advice when about how to pitch to angels like him:

1. The most important thing is the entrepreneur. "Angel investors care more about finding the right entrepreneur than finding the right project."[6]

2. Know thy angel. "Do your research when looking for an angel investor. What type of investments has he made in the past? How well does he know your industry and how strong are his connections within that industry? How did other entrepreneurs feel about working with him? How much time can he devote to you? Have his past investments been successful?"

3. You need to have four presentations ready: (1) the business plan ("no more than 50 pages"); (2) that plan condensed into a PowerPoint (no more than 20 slides); (3) that deck turned into a brief (two pages); (4) that brief condensed into an elevator pitch (five minutes, max).

4. Know the investors' lingo: words like bootstrapping, deals, term sheets, exit strategy, ROI, and valuation.

5. Know what your company's exit strategy is because the angel will want to hear it.

6. Mistakes to avoid: bad presentations, a poor business plan, saying that you need their money but not their expertise, being evasive.

You can swim with the sharks without getting bit if you follow the wise counsel of the sharks themselves; they are literally telling you what and what not to do when making your pitch.

MENTORS

One of the great entrepreneurs of our time is also the greatest point guard in the history of the NBA, Magic Johnson. Magic's basketball career is of course the stuff of legend, but to those in the know, his business career should be too.

Consider:

- While still a player, in 1987, he formed Magic Johnson Enterprises.
- In 1995, he teamed up with Sony to create Magic Johnson Theatres, revolutionizing the movie business and revitalizing inner-city neighborhoods in the process.
- In 1998, Magic teamed up with Starbucks, becoming the only franchisee in Starbucks' history. He later sold his 125 stores at a huge profit.
- In 2001, he partnered with 24 Hour Fitness, opening gyms across the country.
- In 2004, he teamed up with Burger King, eventually opening and owning 29 restaurants.
- In 2012, he joined Guggenheim Baseball Management to help purchase the Los Angeles Dodgers for the then-unheard-of sum of $2 billion.

Not surprisingly, maybe, Magic's official bio on his company website states: "For the last two decades Johnson has consistently *turned heads with his unprecedented partnerships.*" (emphasis added).

So, yes, take it from Magic, teamwork and partnerships are key to creating your own personal small business explosion. But in Magic's case, it has not just been about finding the right partners. For him, it all began with finding the right mentor.

Magic was in his seventh year of his NBA career when he began to take his business dreams seriously. Knowing what he didn't know, he decided that he needed a business mentor. He set up a meeting with Michael Ovitz, the cofounder of one of the most successful talent agencies in the world, Creative Artists Agency, CAA.

Recalls Magic:

> It is a funny story how that meeting came about. During a Lakers game, I was standing on the sidelines getting ready to pass the ball inbounds. There were two businessmen I respect, Peter Guber and Joe Smith, sitting courtside. I looked over and asked, "How do I get into business?" It probably wasn't the best place to ask, but they could tell I was honestly looking for help, so they arranged for me to meet Michael Ovitz.[7]

The meeting did not go as planned:

> Michael dropped a newspaper in front of me. He asked, "When the paper arrives, what do you read first?" I told him I opened the sports section. He looked at me and said, "Wrong answer. From here on, if you want to be involved in business, you have to read business." I walked in his office 6-foot-9 and proud. I left feeling 5-foot-tall and stunned.[8]

Yet, because Magic was a willing, eager, and dedicated student, Ovitz agreed to be his mentor. "I learned that if you want someone to be your mentor, you better be ready to listen and be humbled. I had to prove to him I was serious and that I would listen."

For Magic, that mentorship made all the difference, and it can for you too. Mentors can teach, coach, open doors, make connections, help with funding, and a whole lot more.

To find one, think about people you like and admire, who have businesses you respect, whose success you would like to emulate. Reach out to them. In my experience, people love to be asked and they love to help. Of course, some people are too busy or not interested. No happens, but so too does yes.

This is also where you as mentee come into play. People become mentors because it is their way of giving back, of passing on what they have learned. But the act is not purely idealistic; the mentor needs to get something out of the relationship and experience too. This means that, like Magic Johnson, you have to be open, coachable, and a willing participant. You have to validate for your mentor that he is not wasting his time, and additionally, you'd better be good company!

As with investors and partners, potential mentors are out there in your community. A little chutzpah and a cup of coffee can go a long way.

The other place to find a mentor is an organization I love called SCORE (www.SCORE.org). Think of it as a Peace Corps of businesspeople and entrepreneurs who are ready, willing, and able to coach you, gratis, on just about any business problem you have. 11,000 volunteer counselors strong, SCORE has offices in every state, as well as cities big and small.

Online, SCORE.org is a remarkable resource. You can find your SCORE mentor there and get free coaching, online or off. You can take one of their free small business webinars (you might even find a few by me). There is the Startup Roadmap, blogs and articles, workshops, and a whole lot more.

When it comes to growing your business, mentors can't be beat, and SCORE can't be beat for helping people find those mentors.

BOOM YOUR BUSINESS BOTTOM LINE

▶ Ben needed Jerry. Jobs needed Wozniak. Hewlett needed Packard. Whom do you need?

▶ Partners and joint venturers can be fantastic options for booming your business because they allow you to expand your reach, save you money, and invest in new projects all while giving you access to a person or team with new skills. They fill gaps.

▶ Angel investors, like those on *Shark Tank*, often have expertise the entrepreneur may not have, as well as, of course, capital.

▶ Mentors are another great teammate to consider. You can find one through your network, or online at SCORE.org.

PART V

LIVE LONG
AND PROSPER

Did you know that you have a superpower?
You do.

YOUR SMALL BUSINESS SUPERPOWER

People will forget what you said. They will forget what you did.
But they will never forget how you made them feel.

—Maya Angelou

W hat makes someone fall in love with a business?
I am not talking about love, like "that's a really sweet little place to shop." No, what I am referring to is love as in the business has customers, followers, fans, and friends who believe in it, who root for it, and who rave to others about it.

The question is important because the answer can take our ventures from good to great.

THE APPLE OF MY EYE

Certainly some big businesses evoke that sort of passion. Can you say Apple? That the Cupertino tech giant (it is certainly no longer simply a "computer company") has a devoted fan base is a given, but did you know that Forbes lists Apple as the world's most valuable brand? Google and Microsoft come in a distant second and third.

Why do people love Apple so? There are a myriad of reasons, but it is safe to say that it is a combination of great, intuitive, innovative, user-friendly products, cool design, superb stores, a cohesive, unified ecosystem that works, and not insignificantly in this day and age, values.

That last point, values, is key. *It is when a company has values that align with those of their customers that those customers are most apt to become stark raving fans.* Simon Sinek has a Ted Talk, "How Great Leaders Inspire Action," that has been viewed almost 55 million times in which he explains how this works, and I strongly encourage you to watch it (https://www.ted.com/talks/simon_sinek_how_great_leaders_inspire_action).

The essential idea then is this: Yes, beloved businesses do something great—whatever that thing is that they are supposed to do—but they do something more too. They stand for something that customers can believe in. They connect on some emotional level. They are aligned with their customers' values, forging a personal connection with the customer.

Apple is a perfect example of this because what it does, you can do too.

Let me repeat that. What Apple does, you can do too, and fortunately for you and me, creating the sort of business that fosters a following is actually easier and a lot less expensive for us than it is for Apple.

What are Apple's values? Between its mission statement and its vision statement, Apple's core values come to light. Apple's mission statement is "to bring the best user experience to its customers through its innovative hardware, software, and services." Its vision statement is "We believe that we are on the face of the earth to make great products and that's not changing."

Given this, we see why these values align with those of its customers: Apple is committed to "the best user experience," it innovates, it is design-forward, its products are top quality, it protects user's privacy, and it offers excellent customer service.

Another example of people who fall in love with a business are the many people who have come to embrace Jimmy Buffett's vision of a tropical paradise called Margaritaville. These self-proclaimed "Parrotheads" are passionate about not just Buffett's Caribbean-infused music and concerts, but an entire Margaritaville ecosystem that includes:

- Margaritaville Cafes
- Margaritaville Tequila, Margaritaville Footwear, and a Margaritaville Foods
- The Margaritaville Casino
- "Coral Reefer" brand marijuana
- "Latitude Margaritaville" retirement homes

This empire nets Buffett some $50 million a year, according to *Forbes*.

Why do Parrotheads love all things Buffett? Because the brand is authentic and has values they relate to. It feels personal to them. In an article in InsideHook.com, one of them put the allure this way: "Margaritaville speaks to every age, every background, every gender. It's an inclusive brand of relaxation and positive vibes."[1]

BUYER BEWARE

By the same token, companies that are not in alignment with the values of their customer, who are not relatable and personal, lose those customers. If you look at that same *Forbes* list of top brands, you can also see how ignoring customers' values can be so damaging. The top two brands that lost the most value in 2020 are Facebook—down 21 percent—and Wells Fargo—down 16 percent.

Facebook's issues are almost too numerous to detail, but noteworthy is the fact that a commitment to its users privacy is nonexistent, actual "fake news" continues to proliferate on the site, and its business model of harvesting and selling user data is anathema to many.

Wells Fargo? According to CNN, Wells was the only bank to lose money during the pandemic. In fact, CNN states, "Wells Fargo has gone from one of America's strongest big banks to easily the weakest."[2] If you want to get on the wrong side of customers, just do what Wells Fargo did:

- Wells Fargo had its employees open millions of fake bank and credit card accounts.
- The bank forced thousands of borrowers to pay for auto insurance they did not need.
- Some of those customers had their autos repossessed as a result.
- It imposed unwarranted fees on potential home buyers to lock in mortgage rates.
- And finally, Wells Fargo "has been accused of mistreating workers by retaliating against whistleblowers and forcing employees to work overtime without extra pay."

Righting that ship is proving to be very difficult for that big bank precisely because it is so big. To make a change, large corporations must first agree on the problem, then navigate the bureaucracy, then have a lot of meetings, then create contingencies, then run options up the flagpole, then get buy-in from stakeholders, then institute a response, then monitor the results, and finally, analyze the data.

Turning that giant tanker in a new direction is no trim tab task.

THE LAW OF BUSINESS KARMA

Now, maybe you are thinking that the problems of a couple of Fortune 500 companies don't amount to a hill of beans in this crazy, mixed up world, but you would be wrong. It is the law of business karma: If we listen, trust, and show loyalty, then customers will give us that same love, loyalty, and trust in return. But if we don't, they won't.

> The Colored Girls Museum (TCGM) and the Paul Robeson House & Museum (PRHM) in Philadelphia are two beloved Black and women-led museums. These small but mighty institutions have deep, long-standing relationships with their community, serving as spaces for collective care, community forums, art, and political education.
>
> As has been well-established, African American communities were hit disproportionately hard by COVID-19, and this was even more true for event-based, black-focused institutions like these. Almost overnight in March 2020, both facilities had to shut down, leaving a huge void in the communities they love and serve.
>
> Reopening would not be easy as making both places COVID-19–safe would require a sizable infusion of capital that these nonprofits did not have—for things like air purifiers, protective equipment, cleaning supplies, retrofitting kitchens, and updating outdoor spaces for events.
>
> Flummoxed, scared, but always committed, the two institutions banded together and asked their community for help. It turned out that the community loved them back. A GoFundMe campaign was launched and more than 2,500 people stepped up, digging in and donating $10, $20, $50—whatever they could.
>
> In the end, $108,563 was raised, saving both cherished organizations.

Several years ago, a franchisor in California wanted to discover what its best franchisees had in common. By "best franchisees," it meant those locations that had the lowest employee turnover, the highest revenues, and the most repeat customers. Was it a good location, creative marketing, or what?

To find out, the franchisor hired a company to survey those franchisees. Both in-person and with a written questionnaire, the many franchisees in that vast state gave the company a snapshot of what they were doing right and wrong, and in the process a clear answer to the question emerged.

The company was quite surprised by what it discovered.

It turned out that all of the best franchisees had one thing in common: great bosses.

Digging into the data, the mothership discovered that the best franchisees were owner/operators who were superior leaders. These bosses managed in a friendly, inclusive, participatory way. They gave compliments easily, offered constructive criticism when needed, rewarded a job well done (usually with money, but in other creative ways as well), listened, and created a team that looked out for one another. Employees loved working for these bosses, and it showed.

This then created a cycle of success: Great bosses cultivated happy, loyal employees. In turn, these happy, loyal employees treated customers great, making for happy, loyal customers. And happy, loyal customers became repeat customers.

The success recipe turned out to look like this:

Great boss = happy employees = loyal customers

TRIBES

Seth Godin calls this phenomenon of people emotionally connecting to a business the creation of a "tribe." In his book *Tribes*, he says that two things are necessary for that to occur: a shared interest, and a way to communicate.

Godin gives the example of his first job, when he worked for a small software company called Spinnaker. He was given the task of acquiring science fiction stories and turning them into adventure games. The issue he had was that the company only gave him three part-time programmers and no other staff. What to do?

Godin knew he had to create a tribe of people within the company invested in his success. So, of all things, he launched an internal newsletter.

The newsletter:

> highlighted the work of every person who worked on one of my products. It highlighted their breakthroughs and talked about the new ground we were breaking. Twice a week I talked about our quest. Twice a week I chronicled the amazing work of our tiny tribe. The newsletter connected the tribe members [and] turned a disparate group of career engineers into a working community.

The result was that, "within a month, six engineers defected to the tribe. Then it was 20. Soon, every person in the entire department was either assigned to my project or moonlighting on it."

Why did the engineers join his team? Of course, it was a lot more than a newsletter. "They switched for the journey. They wanted to be part of something that mattered. It was a shared passion." It became personal.

GO SMALL OR GO HOME

You can decide to treat employees well, or not. You can extend that kindness and respect to your team of customers, vendors, investors, employee family members, and the rest of the gang—or not. You can create a culture of love, or not. The choice is yours.

So the first answer then as to why customers fall in love with some businesses but not others is that when you do something they love, they love you for it. The tragedy is when a small business does not realize that it has this ability because it is too preoccupied, or lazy, or mediocre to see it.

Indifference is our kryptonite.

But when you dare to be bold and great, when you are relatable and personal, that is when people will begin to notice and transform from customers into fans.

Kevin Kelly is the founding executive editor of *Wired* magazine. In 2008, he wrote an influential essay that has gone on to be something of a cult classic. Kelly entitled it, "1,000 True Fans." Excerpted, it argues this:

> *To be a successful creator you don't need millions. You don't need millions of dollars or millions of customers, millions of clients or millions of fans. To make a living as a craftsperson, photographer, musician, designer, author, animator, app maker, entrepreneur, or inventor you need only thousands of true fans.*
>
> *These diehard fans will drive 200 miles to see you sing; they will buy the hardback and paperback and audible versions of your book; they will purchase your next [product] sight unseen; they will come to your chef's table once a month.*
>
> *A thousand customers is a whole lot more feasible to aim for than a million fans. Millions of paying fans is not a realistic goal to shoot for. But a thousand fans is doable. If you added one new true fan per day, it'd only take a few years to gain a thousand.*
>
> *The takeaway: Instead of trying to reach the narrow and unlikely peaks of platinum bestseller hits, blockbusters, and celebrity status, you can aim for direct connection with a thousand true fans. On your way, no matter how many fans you actually succeed in gaining, you'll be surrounded not by faddish infatuation, but by genuine and true appreciation.*[3]

CREATING A TRIBE FROM SCRATCH

If anyone knows what it takes to create a passionate, invested small business tribe, it is Joel Comm. On his website (JoelComm.com), he says, "I'm the Functional Futurist. I don't just see the future. I get there first."

That is no mere boast.

I have watched Joel be at the forefront of many trends over the past 30 years (and only sometimes in envy!), often dominating them and always creating a passionate following in the process.

- In what would eventually become Yahoo! Games, Joel created ClassicGames, which he later sold to Yahoo! for $1 million.
- Joel joined Twitter almost at the beginning, in May 2007. He immediately created a massive following, now numbering almost 700,000. He published what would become a bestseller, *Twitter Power*, less than two years later, in January 2009.
- In 2008, he launched an app on the new Apple App Store. Within 14 days, it was ranked first, having been purchased more than 100,000 times.

These days, among other ventures, Joel is the cohost of one of the most popular podcasts about Bitcoin and cryptocurrencies, called *The Bad Crypto Podcast*, as well as the host of another show about non-fungible tokens, NFTs, called *The NiFTy Show*.

I tell you all of these things because I want you to understand that when Joel Comm explains how to create a business that has passionate followers, how to turn casual customers or listeners into devoted fans, we should listen.

How do you do it? He and I sat down for a chat about this very subject. Here's how to do it, in Joel's own words:

> *What I have found is that you start by building a foundation, brick upon brick. Skill upon skill.*
>
> *Next, you need to begin to generate a following. You have to get people to know, like, and trust you. It's about creating a community. Without the foundation of a community it is impossible to take it to the next level because you have yet to achieve the first level.*

This makes a lot of sense, of course; it is like wanting to turn customers into fans without first having customers.

> *I suggest that you choose a medium that works for you,*
> *It could be speaking, writing, video, audio—it does not*
> *really matter. The important thing is that you choose a*
> *platform that you are comfortable with.*

In a previous chapter, we met John Lee Dumas of podcasting fame. John and Joel know one another and at this point in the interview, Joel references John's show, *Entrepreneurs on Fire.*

> *Whatever platform you choose, if you want to go viral*
> *(as it were), you need to be authentic and original. And*
> *you need to add value. People will respond to that. Take*
> *John Lee Dumas for example. His show offers all of*
> *those things. John has a real passion for entrepreneurs,*
> *and his idea of interviewing and celebrating them daily*
> *on a podcast was original. His in-depth interviews and*
> *extras add a lot of value to his listeners.*

The point Joel is making is not insignificant; it is critical. So many people want to "get famous" or "go viral" and they often think it is like a magic trick. A little hocus-pocus and some luck and you can become the next big Instagram influencer. Joel's advice could not be more contra to that. What he says is that you can create loyal customers and convert them into fans through substance, not flash; the hot and trendy alone are fool's gold.

> *When my partner Travis and I launched our "Bad*
> *Crypto" podcast in July of 2017, we just jumped in. We*
> *had both been studying cryptocurrencies, we saw that*
> *there was a dearth of shows about them, and that meant*
> *that there was a market opportunity. So we jumped in.*
> *I cannot emphasize this next point strongly enough:*
> *Everything is storytelling. You have to tell a great story*
> *that is so compelling that other people will want to tell*

it for you. If you do that, they will, and they will become evangelists for the story you are telling and invested in your success.

Artists really get this concept—everything they do tells a story. But business people do not get it. They like to talk about the product and its features. "Blah, blah, blah." Who wants to repeat that? It is when you tell a great story that people will volunteer to share it. People love stories.

Once we decided to do a show about crypto, we took massive action. We jumped in with both feet. And that is the other thing I would suggest—just do it! Whatever it is that you are passionate about, just start. Start talking. Start recording. Start taping.

Record a damn show!

Even if you feel as if you do not have total clarity, the important thing is to just get started. You will figure it out along the way. And if your community can hear your passion and if they get your authenticity, they will respond. They will become your cheerleaders and help to spread the word.

That is how you begin to get a devoted, passionate following, no matter what it is you are doing. It works like this:

Know me, like me, trust me, pay me!

YOUR SMALL BUINESS SUPERPOWER

The small businesses that make the leap from the convenient to the indispensable have a few things in common. Some of these things are obvious: they offer a great product or service, have an excellent team and fair prices, and so on. But the best have something else, something different, something special and extra. They have a *je ne sais quoi* that sets them apart.

What is that mysterious x factor? It is a million tiny things that add up to one big thing. Not content to just be about profit, they really are about making a difference. They are values-driven, they live those values, and those values align with those of their customers and teammates. They tell their unique story in all that they do. They also form deep bonds with their community.

And finally, and most of all, beloved small businesses and the entrepreneurs who run them are aware that they do indeed have a superpower, and they use it wisely:

They take it personally and make it personal.

Using this power, we can chase big dreams, invent, create, do great work, right wrongs, support our teammates, hire rockstars, share good news, cut people slack, instigate, motivate, help friends, deliver on promises, and foster excellence.

We can make a real difference.

You got this!

BOOM YOUR BUSINESS BOTTOM LINE

▶ Great businesses, big and small alike, have values that align with those of their customers. *That* is how a company begins to become beloved.

▶ Another thing great businesses have in common is that they create loyal employees by being great bosses and managers. In turn, those happy employees foster happy customers. The equation is this: Great boss = happy employees = loyal customers.

▶ Creating a tribe is a matter of being authentic, original, passionate, and communicative. Doing so inspires others.

▶ Small businesses do indeed have a superpower. It is their very smallness which allows them to take it personally and make it personal. Do that, make that connection, and people will start to love your business.

▶ When that happens, congratulations. You are creating your own Small Business Boom!

NOTES

CHAPTER 1

1. Sissy Cao, "Mark Cuban Reveals Surprising Coronavirus Business Advice for Entrepreneurs," *The Observer*, June 17, 2020, https://observer .com/2020/06/mark-cuban-coronavirus-economy-prediction-best-time -to-start-company/.
2. "Remote Working Is Here to Stay, But Who Will be Doing It?," World Economic Forum, December 1, 2020, https://www.weforum.org /agenda/2020/12/remote-working-who-will-be-doing-it/.
3. State of Remote Work Report 2019, Owl Labs, https://resources.owllabs .com/state-of-remote-work/2019.

CHAPTER 2

1. Tchiki Davis, "Rewire Your Brain for Happiness by Doing the Opposite," Berkeley Well-Being Institute, https://www.berkeleywellbeing.com /do-the-opposite.html.
2. Brad Tuttle, "Warren Buffett's Boring, Brilliant Vision," *Time*, March 1, 2010.

CHAPTER 3

1. Timothy Ferriss, *The 4-Hour Workweek*, (Crown Publishing, 2009), 362–64.
2. https://www.investopedia.com.

CHAPTER 6

1. Jonah E. Bromwich, "We Asked: Why Does Oreo Keep Releasing New Flavors?" *New York Times*, December 16, 2020.
2. "The Virgin Group," LawAspect.com, https://lawaspect.com/virgin -group-4/.

CHAPTER 7

1. Bitable.com.

2. DiscoverPods.com.
3. Womply.com.
4. https://www.insivia.com/28-video-stats-2018/.
5. Digiday.com.
6. WebTrafficGeeks.org.

CHAPTER 8

1. Steve Strauss, TheSelfEmployed.com, https://www.theselfemployed.com /the-5-guys-fries-trick-that-will-blow-your-mind-and-sales/.

CHAPTER 9

1. https://www.dreamgrow.com/8-reasons-why-your-business-should-use -video-marketing/
2. https://www.hubspot.com/marketing-statistics
3. https://www.forbes.com/sites/forbesagencycouncil/2017/02/03/video -marketing-the-future-of-content-marketing/?sh=2d8a564a6b53

CHAPTER 10

1. AmraandElma.com, https://www.amraandelma.com/our-work/
2. Omnicoreagency.com.
3. Ibid.

CHAPTER 11

1. https://www.politico.com/sponsored-content/2020/11/making-ends -meet.
2. Amazon.
3. BloomReach study.
4. https://www.forbes.com/sites/johnkoetsier/2020/06/12/covid-19 -accelerated-e-commerce-growth-4-to-6-years/?sh=393f2280600f.
5. https://www.politico.com/sponsored-content/2020/11/making-ends -meet.
6. eBay.com

CHAPTER 13

1. Buckminster Fuller, *An Autobiographical Monologue Scenario*, 1980.
2. U.S. Census Bureau.
3. Molly Young, "The Reigning Queen of Pandemic Yoga," *New York Times*, November 25, 2020.
4. www.JoyfullyJobless.com.
5. Catherine LeClair, "How Two Brothers Spotted a Toy Hamster in China and Figured Out How to Make It a Viral Hit in the U.S., Sparking Over One Million in Sales. Here's the Inside Story of How it Happened," *Business Insider*, November 3, 2020.

6. Ibid.

CHAPTER 15

1. Joyce A. Klein, "Bridging the Divide: How Business Ownership Can Help Close the Racial Wealth Gap," FIELD at the Aspen Institute, January 2017, https://assets.aspeninstitute.org/content/uploads/2017/01/Briding-the-Divide.pdf?_ga=2.46173991.1445950950.1591646293-1253535739.1591646293.

CHAPTER 16

1. Rosanna Greenstreet, "How We Met: Ben Cohen and Jerry Greenfield," *Independent*, October 23, 2011.
2. BenJerry.com.
3. Yahoo News, May 22, 2020. https://ph.news.yahoo.com/elton-john-extends-birthday-wishes-long-time-collaborator-055331389.html
4. BCG.com.
5. BBC.com.
6. Steven D. Strauss, *Planet Entrepreneur* (Wiley, 2013).
7. Don Yeager, "Magic Johnson's Fast Break Into Business." *Success Magazine*. July 2, 2010.
8. Ibid.

CHAPTER 17

1. *Why Gen Z Loves Jimmy Buffett*, by Kayla Kibbe, InsideHook, June 17, 2020
2. CNN.com, July 15, 2020.
3. KK.org.

INDEX

ABOUT THE AUTHOR

Steven D. Strauss

MrAllBiz.com

TheSelfEmployed.com

Facebook.com/TheSelfEmployed

@SteveStrauss

Often called "America's leading small business expert," Steve Strauss is one of the world's foremost small business thought leaders. The *USA TODAY* senior small business columnist, Steve is an attorney, entrepreneur, speaker, and influencer. His books have been translated into eight languages, and his *Small Business Bible* is one of the bestselling small business books of all time.

Steve speaks across the country and around the world about small business, entrepreneurship, and global trends in business. Online, his webinars routinely bring in audiences in the thousands. Steve was recently named by SCORE as the leading champion of small business in the United States.

Steve is often tapped to be a corporate spokesperson and brand ambassador for companies such as Visa, Yahoo, PayPal, and Microsoft because they know that his credibility, credentials, expertise, reach, and friendly and intelligent style resonate strongly with entrepreneurs and small business people.

Whether it's blogs, videos, podcasts, live streaming, e-books, webinars, or other digital media, his company, The Strauss Group, creates cutting-edge content for everyone from Fortune 500 companies to small nonprofits. His latest venture is TheSelfEmployed .com.

Finally, Steve's six-figure social media following allows him to regularly tap into his vast tribe of fellow entrepreneurs and small businesses. You can learn more about Steve at MrAllBiz.com, TheSelfEmployed.com, USATODAY.com, or by writing to sstrauss@MrAllBiz.com.